Contents

LIST OF MAPS

The Walking Tours

• • • • • • • • • • • • • •

6th Edition

Haas Mroue

2/07

WILEY

Wiley Publishing, Inc.

Published by:

WILEY PUBLISHING, INC.
111 River St.
Hoboken, NJ 07030-5774

ISBN-13: 978-0-471-77648-2
ISBN-10: 0-471-77648-3

Editor: Risa Weinreb Wyatt
Production Editors: Bethany J. André, Lindsay Thompson
Cartographer: Andrew Murphy
Photo Editor: Richard Fox
Production by Wiley Indianapolis Composition Services

For information on our other products and services or to obtain techni-
cal support, please contact our Customer Care Department within the
U.S. at 800/762-2974, outside the U.S. at 317/572-3993 or fax
317/572-4002.

Wiley also publishes its books in a variety of electronic formats. Some
content that appears in print may not be available in electronic formats.

Manufactured in the United States of America

5   4   3   2   1

About the Author

Haas Mroue studied at the American University of Paris for 2 years before graduating from UCLA Film School. He went on to receive an M.A. in creative writing and literature from the University of Colorado, Boulder. His travel articles, poems, and short stories have appeared in such publications as the *Literary Review,* the *Michigan Quarterly Review, National Geographic,* and *Encyclopaedia Britannica* and have been broadcast on the BBC World Service and Starz! cable TV channel. He's the author of *Frommer's Paris from $95 a Day* and *Frommer's Amsterdam Day by Day,* and a contributor to *Frommer's Europe from $85 a Day, Frommer's Gay & Lesbian Europe, Frommer's South America* and *Frommer's Argentina & Chile.* When he's not on the road, he makes his home on the Olympic Peninsula in Washington.

An Invitation to the Reader

In researching this book, we discovered many wonderful places—hotels, restaurants, shops, and more. We're sure you'll find others. Please tell us about them, so we can share the information with your fellow travelers in upcoming editions. If you were disappointed with a recommendation, we'd love to know that, too. Please write to:

Frommer's Memorable Walks in Paris, 6th Edition
Wiley Publishing, Inc.
111 River St. • Hoboken, NJ 07030-5774

An Additional Note

Please be advised that travel information is subject to change at any time—and this is especially true of prices. We therefore suggest that you write or call ahead for confirmation when making your travel plans. The authors, editors, and publisher cannot be held responsible for the experiences of readers while traveling. Your safety is important to us, however, so we encourage you to stay alert and be aware of your surroundings. Keep a close eye on cameras, purses, and wallets, all favorite targets of thieves and pickpockets.

FROMMERS.COM

Now that you have the guidebook to a great trip, visit our website at **www.frommers.com** for travel information on more than 3,000 destinations. With features updated regularly, we give you instant access to the most current trip-planning information available. At Frommers.com, you'll also find the best prices on airfares, accommodations, and car rentals—and you can even book travel online through our travel booking partners. At Frommers.com, you'll also find the following:

- Online updates to our most popular guidebooks
- Vacation sweepstakes and contest giveaways
- Newsletter highlighting the hottest travel trends
- Online travel message boards with featured travel discussions

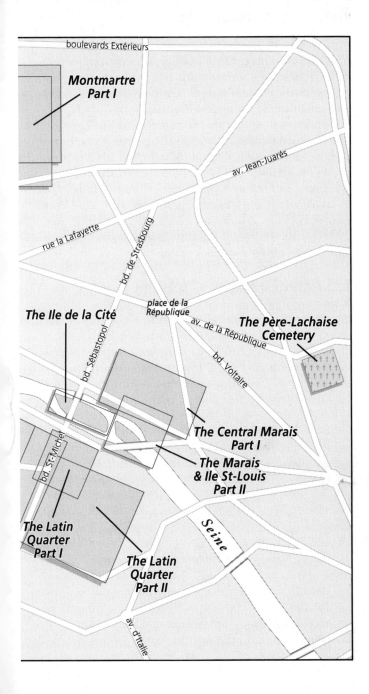

Montmartre
Part I

boulevards Extérieurs

av. Jean-Juarès

rue la Lafayette

bd. de Strasbourg

place de la
République

av. de la République

The Ile de la Cité

The Père-Lachaise
Cemetery

bd. Sébastopol

bd. Voltaire

The Central Marais
Part I

The Marais
& Ile St-Louis
Part II

bd. St-Michel

The Latin
Quarter
Part I

The Latin
Quarter
Part II

Seine

av. d'Italie

the 13th century. The *bouquinistes* (booksellers) along the Seine have plied their trade there for almost 400 years. And even in commercialized St-Germain you'll find the bookstores, publishing houses, theaters, and galleries that have made this district an intellectual hot spot for centuries.

And then there's the physical beauty of the city. The sheer variety of architectural styles is staggering—everything from a 15th-century cottage in the south Marais to the fabulous mansions in the faubourg St-Germain. In certain parts of Paris, you'll genuinely feel as if you're stepping into a painting. In Montmartre, for example, you can walk through rustic lanes painted by Utrillo or gaze upon a windmill painted by Renoir. In the Marais, the rows of elegantly designed and ornamented houses make a kind of urban sculpture.

THE NEIGHBORHOOD LOWDOWN

Which walks you decide to take—and in what order—depends on your time and interest, but I have organized them chronologically in order to trace Paris's historical and cultural development. For the first 1,400 years, **Ancient and Medieval Paris** centered around the Ile de la Cité and the Latin Quarter. When Charles V moved his court to the Right Bank in the 14th century, the Marais and Ile St-Louis emerged as the heart of **Royal Paris,** but in the 18th century the aristocracy moved on to the faubourg St-Germain. In the 19th century, artists, writers, and intellectuals began gravitating to St-Germain, and in the 20th century they spread to Montmartre and Montparnasse. The walks through **Literary and Artistic Paris** pass the studios, apartments, and watering holes of the city's most illustrious residents. You can then pay them your respects at the cemeteries of Montmartre and Montparnasse and at the splendid Père-Lachaise.

As you'll see, Paris grew in a series of concentric circles radiating from the original nucleus on the **Ile de la Cité.** Lying just about in the geographical center of the city, this fascinating island contains 2,000 years of French history. From traces of the original Gallo-Roman settlement to the soaring Notre-Dame and Sainte-Chapelle, you can see reminders of an earlier Paris. The quiet medieval streets next to Notre-Dame recall the religious and scholarly life that flourished there, yet the other side of this island is anything but contemplative.

Lawyers dash in and out of the Palais de Justice, tourists swarm around the two churches, and Parisians on various administrative missions fill the Préfecture.

The **Latin Quarter,** on the Left Bank of the Seine, was settled by the Romans immediately after their conquest of the Ile de la Cité. Vestiges of this era dot the neighborhood, most notably at the Musée de Cluny's Roman baths and the Arènes de Lutèce (arena) in the south; still, most of what you'll see stems from Paris's medieval days as a center of learning. Cobblestone streets and alleys wind around the monumental structures that headquarter the great Université de Paris at the Sorbonne. This lively district still throngs with students today, and many of the cafes and shops retain a suitably rumpled, bohemian allure.

While the churches were appearing on the Left Bank, the Right Bank was becoming the home of royalty. In the 14th century, Charles V moved from his château on the Ile de la Cité to the **Marais,** and the neighborhood blossomed for 4 centuries. On your walk, you'll see 17th-century aristocratic mansions called *hôtels particuliers,* built during the full flower of French architecture and sculpture. The central Marais has been reborn as an active and fashionable neighborhood with boutiques, galleries, and restaurants. It's also the center of Paris's gay life.

When the restless aristocracy moved from the Marais in the 18th century, they settled farther west in the **faubourg St-Germain.** The noble families were flush with money, and it seems that a good part of it was spent here. The lavish manors now house embassies and government ministries; when the nine-to-fivers leave, the neighborhood quiets down considerably. In the midst of all the official business are two world-class museums: the Musée d'Orsay and Musée Rodin.

The 1789 revolution interrupted the spending spree, and the subsequent rise of Napoléon Bonaparte began a war spree. Once the smoke cleared, Paris emerged as the international capital of art and literature, a position that it held for more than a century. From the mid–19th century to the mid–20th century, the artistic and intellectual community moved among St-Germain, Montparnasse, and Montmartre.

With its abundance of bookstores and the world-class Ecole des Beaux-Arts, 19th-century **St-Germain,** east of the faubourg St-Germain, became a prime area for artists and intellectuals. The arrival of American expatriate writers in the early 20th century was followed by a burst of excitement after World War II, when Jean-Paul Sartre and Simone de Beauvoir presided over a flock of existentialist disciples in the cafes on boulevard St-Germain. The intellectual ferment has since abated, and today the literary cafes attract more foot-weary visitors than philosophers or Parisians. The neighborhood retains a tremendous vitality, however, and offers a full range of activities—from shops to restaurants to jazz clubs.

In the late 19th century, the cabarets and country lanes of **Montmartre** began to lure painters away from St-Germain and the conservative Ecole des Beaux-Arts. Van Gogh, Renoir, Degas, Toulouse-Lautrec, Seurat, and Utrillo all found inspiration in both the daylight and the nightlife of this village on a hill. Even before World War I, the artists of Montmartre were being edged out by visitors, a transition that's now complete. The leafy streets and spectacular views over Paris remain as enchanting as ever, even if the Impressionist masters have been replaced by hectoring quick-sketch artists.

Montparnasse reached the height of its popularity during the inter-war period, when Chagall, Picasso, and Modigliani were joined by American expatriates in the cafes along boulevard Montparnasse. Cafe society deserted Montparnasse during World War II, however, and the area hasn't been the same since. The vast shopping-and-entertainment complex around the Montparnasse train station has produced a carnival-like atmosphere that feels inconsistent with Montparnasse's literary and artistic past. At least the grand old cafes are still going strong, now drawing an intriguing mix of Left Bank eccentrics, American visitors, Japanese businessmen, gigolos, and models.

Part of the joy of strolling through Paris is discovering the city's secrets. Whenever possible, I've planned these walks to take you off the beaten track, through half-hidden passages, and into secluded parks and gardens. Some architectural delights are tucked behind massive doors or gates. Though an increasing number of courtyards and passages are closed to the public, you can enter many on weekdays simply by pressing a buzzer on the side to open the door.

Even well-worn tourist routes hold clues to the city's past. Certain buildings still boast the insignia of 16th-century shops on their facades or the medieval name of the street engraved on the sides. A pattern of paving stones can help you to visualize a vanished neighborhood or an ancient wall.

While exploring, you'll enter into the lives of the famous, non-famous, and infamous characters that made modern Paris. You'll read stories of womanizing kings, treacherous queens, bankrupt dukes, murderous feuds, brilliant artists, grand passions, and grand crimes. More important, you'll come to understand how the daily life of ordinary Parisians produced such an extraordinarily rich culture. Spend the afternoon over a coffee in a street-corner cafe and you'll understand why cafes were good places to plot revolutions or hatch complicated new philosophies. Watch a matron cross-examine a butcher in a street market and you'll see how Paris became a culinary capital. The gift for visual expression that culminates in a Monet or a Renoir displays itself everywhere. The lusciously arranged shop windows, the flowers that pour over iron balconies, the meandering streets of individually crafted houses compose an urban landscape of exquisite beauty and grace. *Ça, c'est Paris!*

HISTORY 101: FROM LUTECE TO THE CITY OF LIGHT

Because the history of Paris is inextricably linked with the growth of its diverse neighborhoods, the introduction to each walk contains a more detailed discussion. The following overview should give you a broad idea of the forces that shaped the city you'll be exploring.

Paris's geographic location was ideal for the development of a metropolis. The Seine provided transportation to outlying regions and irrigated a large swath of land. The Atlantic Ocean was also within reach, providing a source of seafood and access to far-flung lands rich in resources. The fertile soil and favorable climate could produce enough food to sustain a large population. And beneath the ground were vast deposits of limestone and gypsum (plaster of Paris) to construct buildings.

For the earliest Parisians, the topography wasn't a problem; other people were. The tribe that migrated to the area around the 3rd century B.C. chose the most defensible position that it could find: an island in the middle of the Seine, now known as the Ile de la Cité. Nevertheless, they were no match for the Roman army that conquered the island in 52 B.C. and named it Lutetia Parisorum (*Lutèce* in French).

The Romans settled in for about 4 centuries, during which time they constructed roads, baths, and an arena on the Left Bank. A Gallo-Roman wall was built on the Ile de la Cité, the first of a series of defensive fortifications to protect Paris. Both pagan and Roman gods were worshiped in temples, which later became sanctuaries for the early Christians.

The 5th-century fall of Rome ushered in a dark, confusing epoch for Lutèce, brightened only by the decision of King Clovis in 508 to make his capital at the city he now called Paris. The incessant threat of Norman attacks finally subsided in the 9th century when the marauders were driven away for good by Count Eudes. In the ensuing peace, two powerful forces emerged that shaped Paris's development for 800 years: the monarchy and the church.

The first Capetian kings established their palace on the Ile de la Cité, which was also the site of numerous churches. With the construction of Notre-Dame and the king's palace, Ile de la Cité became the populous hub of 12th- and 13th-century Paris. Meanwhile, a series of village settlements began to form around several abbeys on the Right and Left banks. In 1190, Philippe-Auguste ordered a new wall begun to encircle the island and the villages along the banks of the Seine.

By the 14th century, the monarchy and the church were regarding each other from opposite sides of the river. The Left Bank abbeys increased in prestige as they attracted renowned scholars and theologians. A powerful university, the Sorbonne, developed in the Latin Quarter under the auspices of the church. The Right Bank had become a busy port, with a large market on the site of the current Forum des Halles shopping center. When Charles V moved to the Marais, it sprang to life as a residential district. He built another wall to protect his royal enclave. Ambitious people of wealth and privilege naturally wished to be closer to the king's court, and so the Marais flourished—until, of course, the royal family left.

After the 1610 assassination of Henri IV, his widow, Marie de Médici, and her son, Louis XIII, moved west to the Louvre. Louis saw to it that Charles V's wall was extended westward to include the Palais du Louvre and the Tuileries. His brilliant and ruthless minister, Cardinal Richelieu, built the Palais Cardinal (now the Palais Royal) nearby, and the aristocracy began drifting west to the prestigious new neighborhood.

The Left Bank remained the territory of abbeys and schools until Louis XIV moved to his palace at Versailles in the mid–17th century. Those who had business with the king, but weren't invited to live at court, shortened their travel time to Versailles by relocating southwest to the faubourg St-Germain, a suburb of the St-Germain-des-Prés abbey. By this time, the kingdom was secure enough for Louis to tear down the old walls; in their place, wide new boulevards were laid out, among them boulevards des Capucines, des Italiens, and de la Madeleine.

The wall-free period ended with the construction of the *fermiers généraux* (farmer generals) wall in 1784; the barrier was designed to allow a group of wealthy financiers to charge hefty import taxes on commodities such as salt and wine. This hated wall became one of the insults to the common people that helped incite the French Revolution just a few years afterward; it was eventually demolished several decades later, along with most of the tollgates.

After the revolution, the church and the aristocracy no longer dictated the development of neighborhoods, and a new force grew in their place: the bourgeoisie. After the Napoleonic Wars ended with Bonaparte's 1814 defeat at Waterloo, the population of Paris increased from little more than 500,000 to a stunning 2,270,000 in 1881. The industrial age arrived along with the railroads, and the city needed reshaping.

Modern Paris emerged under Napoléon III. His Préfet de la Seine, Baron Georges-Eugène Haussmann, devised a system of crossroads around place de l'Opéra and place de l'Etoile and created boulevards to link the four grand rail stations. More boulevards were laid out along the former *fermiers généraux* wall. Entire neighborhoods were razed, their unfortunate populations displaced to the east; the wealthy classes continued their march westward to the area around the Champs-Elysées, the faubourg St-Honoré, and the villages of Auteuil and Passy, now in the 16th arrondissement.

In 1860, the legislature passed a law annexing the villages that lay just outside the *fermiers généraux* walls and instituting the administrative system of arrondissements. Of the 20 arrondissements, roughly the 12th through the 20th are composed of previously independent villages, such as Montmartre, that acquired the right to pay taxes to the city of Paris in exchange for improvements in hygiene and urbanization.

The bloodshed and turmoil of the World Wars left Paris largely untouched (at least physically), but in the latter half of the 20th century, the city modernized with impressive speed. Traffic circulation improved with the addition of roads along the Seine and around the city's perimeter. Vast sums were spent on projects like the office center at La Défense, the science center at La Villette, the Pompidou Centre library and museum, the Cité de la Musique, the Forum des Halles shopping center, the Institut du Monde Arabe, the Opéra Bastille, and I. M. Pei's controversial glass pyramid at the Louvre. The most recent project is the construction of the Bibliothèque Nationale de France in the Bercy neighborhood near the Gare d'Austerlitz. It's hoped that this plan will revitalize Paris's neglected southeast section.

The population in the 20 arrondissements stands at about 2.2 million, but the greater Parisian metropolis (including the surrounding *départements*) is now home to more than 10 million people. Low-cost housing is scarce in central Paris, and the postwar years have seen a steady exodus of the working class out of Paris and into the suburbs. The centuries-old westward movement of the privileged classes has made the western arrondissements and suburbs far more upscale than those to the east.

The more run-down neighborhoods in the east have long been home to immigrants from France's former colonies in Africa and southeast Asia, but the low rents have recently begun attracting struggling artists as well. Whether the troubled east Paris neighborhoods contain the seeds of a cultural revival remains to be seen, but the City of Light has demonstrated a remarkable ability to mold itself around the aspirations of each new generation.

The Ile de la Cité

Start: Place Louis-Lépine (Métro: Cité).

Finish: Square du Vert-Galant.

Time: 3 to 5 hours, depending on how much time you spend in the churches and museums.

Best Time: Any time during the day.

Worst Time: Major holidays, when the Conciergerie and Sainte-Chapelle are closed.

T here's no better place to begin exploring Paris than the Ile de la Cité, the city's historical, spiritual, and administrative center. It was here that the earliest Parisians settled more than 2,000 years ago. It was here that Roman and then French monarchs established rule. The soaring towers of Notre-Dame and the massive windows of Sainte-Chapelle proclaim the glory of Gothic art, while France's judicial and administrative systems remain firmly centered on the island where it all originated.

The Ile de la Cité was ideally situated for the Germanic Parisii tribe that arrived in the 3rd century B.C. The Seine formed a natural moat to protect the tribe's settlement and was an abundant source of fish. The Parisii produced excellent boatmen who traded up and down the river with neighboring tribes, a nearly forgotten chapter in the city's history that is recalled in the city's coat of arms: a boat with the Latin inscription FLUCTUAT NEC MERGITUR ("It floats and does not sink"). Their settlement was also conveniently located on the main north–south trading route connecting the Mediterranean with northern Europe.

That was the good news. The bad news was that the river and the road made handy routes for invaders, not just traders. The island was repeatedly attacked, first and most successfully by the Romans. Julius Caesar stormed through France in 52 B.C. after defeating the Gallic leader Vercingétorix, and quickly made the Parisii settlement an urban outpost of his Empire. The Romans found the city so agreeable that they stayed for 500 years, and the settlement became known as Lutetia Parisiorum (*Lutèce* in French). They built a temple to Jupiter on the site of Notre-Dame, put administrative buildings where the parvis is now, and installed their governor at the site of the current Palais de Justice. Until the 17th century, the western end of the Palais de Justice marked the limit of the island. Place Dauphine and square du Vert-Galant were created in 1607 by fastening two smaller islands to the Ile de la Cité.

Barbarians came in 276, and a population that had expanded to the Left Bank took shelter on the island and built a wall to protect itself. Attila and the Huns were next on the scene in 451; according to legend, only the help of Geneviève, Paris's patron saint, saved the city. In 486, France began to stabilize as an independent kingdom when the first Merovingian king, Clovis, defeated the last Roman governor and turned back the Visigoths and Alemanni.

In 508, Clovis made Paris his capital, and the island became known as the Ile de la Cité. Christianity took root under the Merovingian monarchs, and two grand churches were built near the royal palace: St-Etienne and the first Notre-Dame. The Carolingians succeeded the Merovingians, and Paris was subject to repeated Norman invasions. When the Carolingian dynasty ended in 987, the nobles chose as king

The Ile de la Cité

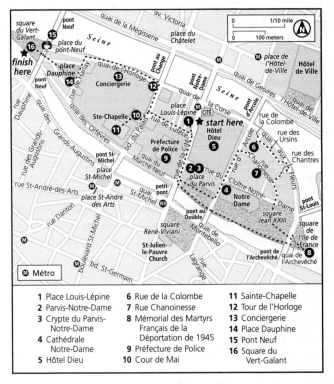

Métro

1 Place Louis-Lépine
2 Parvis-Notre-Dame
3 Crypte du Parvis-Notre-Dame
4 Cathédrale Notre-Dame
5 Hôtel Dieu
6 Rue de la Colombe
7 Rue Chanoinesse
8 Mémorial des Martyrs Français de la Déportation de 1945
9 Préfecture de Police
10 Cour de Mai
11 Sainte-Chapelle
12 Tour de l'Horloge
13 Conciergerie
14 Place Dauphine
15 Pont Neuf
16 Square du Vert-Galant

Hugh Capet, comte de Paris and duc de France, beginning the new Capetian dynasty. His successors resided on the Ile de la Cité until the 14th century, and the island became the center of royal and ecclesiastical power. The kings and their administration occupied the eastern part, where the Palais de Justice now stands, while the remainder became crowded with churches and houses. The powerful canons of Notre-Dame established a school in the 11th century, attracting scholars from all over Europe to the bustling island.

Many of the famous sights here are the legacy of the Capetians. Notre-Dame was begun under Louis VII in 1193, Louis IX completed Sainte-Chapelle in 1248, and much of the Conciergerie dates from the 14th-century reign of Philippe le Bel. Charles V was the last king to live on the island; after the uprising led by Etienne Marcel, he retreated to safer quarters on the Right Bank.

Even without the kings, the island continued to flourish as Parliament took over the royal residence. Fires were frequent, and the palace was rebuilt several times before the revolution. The revolutionaries renamed it the Palais de Justice and set up their Tribunal within its halls. The targets of their wrath were judged in the Tribunal and held in the Conciergerie before, in most cases, being hauled off to the guillotine.

Much of what you'll see on this walk dates from the mid–19th century, when Baron Haussmann, the prefect of Paris, swept through with his team of urban planners and remade the island. The neglected jewels, Notre-Dame and Sainte-Chapelle, were polished up; the Palais de Justice was extended; and the medieval Hôtel Dieu was torn down and replaced with the current one. Also razed was a full three-quarters of the medieval neighborhood, a particularly lamentable decision.

The many courts and tribunals installed in and around the Palais de Justice ensure that the center of the island hums with activity on weekdays. Even in off-hours, crowds of visitors mill around Notre-Dame, Sainte-Chapelle, and the Conciergerie. This walk will also take you to the island's quieter side. The triangular place Dauphine and the square du Vert-Galant on the tip make ideal rest stops, and the nearly empty quarter north of Notre-Dame evokes the vanished world of medieval clerics and scholars.

• • • • • • • • • • • • • • • •

When you come out of the Cité Métro station, you'll be on:

1. **Place Louis-Lépine,** facing the flower market held Monday to Saturday 8am to 6pm. The potted plants, shrubs, and fresh flowers add a welcome touch of nature to the stone-and-concrete center of the island. Sundays 8am to 7pm the flower market becomes a bird market, carrying on a long tradition of bird sellers in Paris.

   If you have kids in tow, you may want to linger awhile here admiring the hundreds of bird cages and their colorful (and chirpy) occupants.

   Then go all the way through the market toward the Seine, bearing right, and you'll end up on the corner of rue de la Cité. Turn right and walk a block to the:

2. **Parvis-Notre-Dame.** Enjoy the view of the magnificent cathedral across the square (a *parvis* is a square in front of a church). Until the 19th century, a network of medieval streets and buildings nearly obscured the cathedral. Then Baron Haussmann cleared the parvis of thousands of inhabitants as well as their houses, churches, and cabarets. The outline of this old neighborhood and its main street, rue de Neuve Notre-Dame, is traced in colored paving stones on the parvis.

Underneath the parvis is the:

3. **Crypte du Parvis-Notre-Dame.** In 1965, excavations for a new parking lot under the parvis revealed Gallo-Roman ramparts, 3rd-century rooms heated by an underground furnace system called a hypocaust, and cellars of medieval houses. Naturally, the parking lot idea was abandoned and the excavations were turned into an archaeological museum. When you go down to the crypt, you'll be at the island's original level. Throughout the centuries, builders erected new structures over the ruins of previous settlements, raising the Ile de la Cité about 7m (23 ft.). To help you visualize the kinds of buildings that once stood here, there are scale models showing how Paris grew from a small settlement to a Roman city, as well as photographs of the pre-Haussmann parvis. The crypt is open daily except Monday 10am to 6pm (10am–5pm in winter), and there's an admission fee.

Emerge from the crypt and head toward Notre-Dame. To your right is a **statue of Charlemagne** from about 1882.

In 1768, it was announced that a spot at the far end of place du Parvis, in front of Notre-Dame, would be the point from which all road distances to Paris would be measured. And so it came to pass, and today a circular bronze plaque marks *kilomètre zéro.*

Continue on to the:

4. **Cathédrale Notre-Dame.** Like many Gothic cathedrals, Notre-Dame was built on a site that had been considered holy for many centuries. This is where the Romans built a temple to Jupiter, the remains of which were found in 1711. In 528, the Merovingian king

Childebert built the first Notre-Dame here using stones from the Roman arena on the Left Bank. By the 11th century, this church and the neighboring St-Etienne were falling apart; at the same time, the population of Paris was growing. In 1160, Maurice de Sully, the bishop of Paris, had an idea to build one immense church to replace the two older ones. Three years later, work began on this cathedral, which took almost 200 years to complete; construction ended in 1359.

The facade's design is perfectly proportioned, deftly balancing space and stone, the vertical and the horizontal. The two towers are narrower at the top than at the base, lending them the illusion of great height. The central door is larger than the others, and the one on the left has a gable, introducing an asymmetry that enhances the overall harmony. Beneath the rose window over the main entrance are 28 statues of the kings of Judea and Israel that were smashed by 18th-century revolutionaries under the mistaken impression that the statues represented French kings. They were restored in the 19th century by Viollet-le-Duc.

The cathedral interior also fell victim to revolutionary fervor: Few of the original furnishings remain today because Notre-Dame was pillaged. Sometime during the revolutionary period, the stained-glass windows were also replaced with clear glass and the walls whitewashed. It wasn't until the 1830s that anyone thought about restoring the cathedral. Victor Hugo's *Hunchback of Notre-Dame* (1831) played a large role in generating public interest in the church and, finally, stimulated Louis-Philippe to order a restoration project in 1844.

Try to visit Notre-Dame on a sunny day, when light streams through the rose windows. The north rose window, representing Old Testament prophets and kings, has remained nearly intact since the 13th century. The remarkable lightness of its design is due to the then-new ability of 13th-century artisans to create windows with more glass than stone. Look for the Coustou and Coysevox sculptures in the choir; Robert de Cotte's choir stalls, on the backs of which are bas-reliefs, including scenes depicting the Virgin Mary's life; and Cliquot's organ (1730). You should also climb the tower and take

Baron Haussmann: The Man Who Transformed Paris

Baron Georges-Eugène Haussmann created so much of the Paris we see today that it's impossible to ignore him. Given the job by Napoléon III, he transformed the city in the 1850s and 1860s from a medieval town into a 19th-century metropolis. He razed old Paris, widened the streets, and laid out a series of broad boulevards leading from four then-new rail stations on the city's periphery into its heart. Along their routes he created dramatic open spaces such as place de l'Opéra and place de l'Etoile (now place Charles-de-Gaulle–Etoile).

Haussmann was born in Paris in 1809 and went to the provinces, where he gained a reputation as a tough administrator. In 1853, Napoléon III appointed him Préfet de la Seine, and Haussmann began the work of revising Paris. His lack of tact and obstinate conviction in his superiority were notorious, and he was widely hated for the destruction he caused. Although his actions swept away many of the densest old neighborhoods filled with mansions and private gardens, the straight broad avenues he created did modernize the city and make it more navigable.

The Haussmann boulevards are lined with buildings of a relatively uniform pattern. Typically, they're seven stories tall, built of limestone with long wrought-iron balconies on the second, fifth, and sixth floors. The top floor usually contains irregularly shaped apartments or garrets intended as servants' quarters for the bourgeois families who occupied the lower floors. Today these tiny *chambres des bonnes* (maids' rooms) are relatively inexpensive lodgings for those priced out of expensive Paris real estate.

in Paris from above—the view is unparalleled. The entrance is outside, to the right.

Throughout the ages, Notre-Dame has served as Paris's community hall. Extravagant banquets were thrown open to the people; plays were staged in front of the doors; and curiosities, such as elephant tusks and whale's ribs, were displayed inside.

The church was a sanctuary for the poor, the weary, and fugitives from justice. Philippe le Bel once rode inside on horseback, and it was here in 1430 that Henri VI of England was crowned king. In 1779, Louis XIV dowered 100 young women and married them off here en masse. In 1793, a belly dancer was placed on the high altar, and the saints in the niches were replaced by statues of the likes of Voltaire and Rousseau. And it was here in 1804 that Napoléon Bonaparte, usurping the role of Pope Pius VII, lifted the imperial crown from the altar and crowned himself emperor and Joséphine empress.

Notre-Dame was constructed as an expression of profound religious faith, and the sheer beauty and force of the building—with its sculpture-encrusted facade, leering gargoyles, and flying buttresses (which date from the 14th c.)—have made it perhaps the highest single artistic achievement of the Gothic period.

When you leave the cathedral, go right and you'll see the entrance to the:

5. **Hôtel Dieu,** across the street on rue du Cloître Notre-Dame. Built by Diet from 1866 to 1878 in neo-Florentine style, the Hôtel Dieu is the main hospital for central Paris, replacing the original 12th-century Hôtel Dieu that had run the entire width of the island, touching both riverbanks. The location of the medieval hospital may have been chosen for its proximity to Notre-Dame. (With a mortality rate of 20% in those days, patients needed all the help they could get—both divine and medical.) Or it may have been placed conveniently close to the Seine in order that the water would flush away hospital waste. Go in the main entrance and take a break in the spacious neoclassical courtyard, whose small garden and fountain make a quiet oasis on this busy island.

From rue du Cloître Notre-Dame, make a left on rue d'Arcole. The entire area from here to the eastern tip of the island was once occupied by the cloister of Notre-Dame, a small city-within-a-city of winding streets and three-story half-timbered houses. It was here that Notre-Dame's canons established a prestigious school where scholars like Pierre Abélard (see Walking Tour 7, Stop 7) and Maurice de Sully taught the sons of kings. Fortunately, the neighborhood was spared Haussmann's restructuring due to the baron's death. Though much has been renovated beyond recognition, the narrow interior streets I'll lead you down retain a flavor of medieval Paris.

From rue d'Arcole, make a right onto rue Chanoinesse and then a left onto:

6. **Rue de la Colombe,** dating from the 13th century. At **no. 6,** the traces of the 3rd-century Gallo-Roman wall are outlined in colored paving stones on the street, and at **no. 4,** a medieval door topped with a medallion of two doves *(colombes)* recalls the St-Nicolas tavern that stood here in the 13th century.

Continue on to **rue des Ursins,** turn right, and notice **no. 7,** the 17th-century house where playwright Jean Racine allegedly lived. Follow the street to rue des Chantres and turn right onto:

7. **Rue Chanoinesse,** scene of the crime of the century— the 14th century, that is. Somewhere on this street (the exact addresses are unknown) were the adjoining shops of a barber and a baker, the latter renowned for the excellence of his pâtés. At the time, the neighborhood was packed with students, many of them foreign. If one disappeared every so often, it was assumed that he fell victim to one of the muggers and thieves who plied the area. But when a German student vanished one day in 1387, his dog began barking furiously in front of the barbershop. No one could get the dog away from the shop, so police were called. After an interrogation we may assume was forceful, the barber finally confessed that for years he had been slitting the throats of students and selling the bodies to the neighboring patisserie. Both culprits were placed in an iron cage and burned alive, and their grisly story became the subject of a popular medieval song.

Look for **nos. 22** and **24,** excellent examples of 16th-century gabled canonical houses. The entry hall of **no. 26** is paved with tombstones (gray slabs, no engravings), probably from one of the many church cemeteries that dotted the island. A buzzer opens the door any day except Sunday. Retrace your steps and notice the well-preserved 17th-century facade of the **Hôtel du Grand Chantre** at **no. 12. No. 10** is thought to be the location of the house of Héloïse's uncle, where she and Abélard fell in love (see Walking Tour 7, Stop 7).

Follow rue Chanoinesse to the entrance to **square Jean XXIII,** where you'll see restrooms on your right. This stately park is usually busy with people enjoying a magnificent view of the cathedral's east end. The 14th-century flying buttresses stretch like graceful tentacles from the apse that joins Viollet-le-Duc's 90m (295-ft.) spire. The park is on the site of the archbishop's residence, built in the 17th century and destroyed during a riot in 1831. The square opened in 1844; at its center is the neo-Gothic fountain known as Fontaine de la Vierge.

Go to the tip of the square and cross quai de l'Archevêché, heading into square de l'Ile de France, to reach the haunting:

8. **Mémorial des Martyrs Français de la Déportation de 1945.** Descend the stairs (you'll see the iron spikes blocking the opening at the tip of the island), then turn left at the bottom, and pass through the narrow opening. Designed by G.H. Pingusson in 1962, the memorial is dedicated to the 200,000 French who died in Nazi concentration camps during World War II. The concrete, iron spikes, and claustrophobic rooms vividly convey a sensation of imprisonment. One room is constructed around 200,000 quartz pebbles—in the Jewish religion it's traditional to place a stone or pebble on a grave, and there's one pebble here for each person who died. Also inside are several other small tombs holding bits of soil from each of the concentration camps.

Retrace your steps across quai de l'Archevêché but, for variety, walk on the left side of square Jean XXIII, which affords a view of the tree-lined Left Bank. Cross rue d'Arcole, continuing on the left side of Parvis-Notre-Dame, and make a right on rue de la Cité. On your left is the:

9. **Préfecture de Police.** Here in the Palais de la Cité's old barracks, the police joined the Resistance against the

Nazis in 1944 by twice locking themselves inside—first
on August 19, then on August 26. Almost 300 were
killed.

Head back toward the Cité Métro station. You'll come
to a wide pedestrian street, rue de Lutèce. Turn left and
head toward the elaborate Louis XVI wrought-iron gate
separating boulevard du Palais from the:

10. **Cour du Mai.** The May Courtyard took its name from
an old custom in which clerks of the court planted a tree
there every May 1 (though you won't find any trees here
now). The buildings around it were constructed between
1783 and 1787, on the site of the old Merovingian palace
that was destroyed by fires in 1618 and 1776. During the
revolution, crowds used to gather on the steps in front of
the courtyard to watch victims of the Reign of Terror pass
from the yard on the right, which abuts the Conciergerie,
to carts waiting to take them to the guillotine at place de
la Révolution (now place de la Concorde). The steps lead
to the **Palais de Justice,** Paris's law-court complex stretching from boulevard du Palais to place Dauphine. The
courts that Balzac described as a "cathedral of chicanery"
are open to the public, with the entrance to the left of the
great gate. Here you'll also find the entrance to:

11. **Sainte-Chapelle.** This chapel, the oldest part of the
Palais de Justice complex, was built between 1246 and
1248 by Louis IX to house two significant religious artifacts: a piece of the cross on which Christ was said to have
been crucified, and what may be the Crown of Thorns
(both have been moved to Notre-Dame and are on view
only on Good Friday). It's said that, to acquire these artifacts, St. Louis paid nearly triple the amount required for
the entire church's construction.

Sainte-Chapelle really consists of two chapels, one on
top of the other. The *chapelle basse* (lower chapel) was
used by palace servants and is ornamented with fleur-de-
lis designs. The *chapelle haute* (upper chapel) is one of the
highest achievements of Gothic art. Although the painted
columns and much of the sculptures date from the 19th
century, two-thirds of the stained-glass windows are original, most from the 13th century. Old and New

Testament scenes are emblazoned in 15 perfect stained-glass windows covering 612 sq. m (nearly 6,600 sq. ft.). The 1,134 scenes trace the Christian story from the Garden of Eden to the Apocalypse, and you read them from bottom to top and from left to right. The first window to the right represents the story of the Crown of Thorns; St. Louis is shown several times. Some of the windows show the church's construction, and the great Rose Window is meant to depict the Apocalypse.

Go left to quai de l'Horloge to see the:

12. **Tour de l'Horloge,** the site of Paris's first public clock, built in 1371 and restored many times. The frame is emblazoned with the royal fleurs-de-lis, and the figures represent Justice on the right and Law on the left. The clock no longer works.

Around the corner at **no. 1** quai de l'Horloge is the:

13. **Conciergerie,** much of which was built by Philippe le Bel in the 14th century as an extension of the Capetian palace. The Salle des Gardes and Salle des Gens d'Armes are particularly fine examples of secular Gothic architecture. Later, this building's prisons were used as holding cells for the revolution's tribunals. Marie Antoinette was held here before her execution; others imprisoned here before execution included Robespierre and Danton. Exactly 4,164 "enemies of the people" passed through the Conciergerie between January 1793 and July 1794, more than half of them headed for the guillotine.

Continue along quai de l'Horloge and first you'll see the **Tour de César,** where Ravaillac, Henri IV's assassin, was held and probably tortured. Next is the **Tour d'Argent,** where the crown jewels were stored at one time. Both towers were built around 1300. The **Tour de Bonbec** is the last and oldest tower, built around 1250. It was called *bonbec* ("babbler") because the torture inflicted here was so intense. Prisoners had their legs squeezed between two planks or ropes tied progressively tighter around different parts of their bodies until they cut into the skin. The oldest form of torture was a trap door that opened into a pit of razor-sharp spikes. You'd babble, too.

Including the Tour de l'Horloge, these four towers are the only remains of the Capetian palace and were restored in the 19th century. Notice how the facade of the Conciergerie changes from a Gothic style to a Corinthian style as you walk west along the quai.

Turn left on **rue de Harlay** and notice the Louis XIII facade at **no. 2.** On your right is the restful:

14. **Place Dauphine,** another of Henri IV's successful projects. The king who ended the religious wars was also Paris's first urban planner. After designing the royal place des Vosges (see Walking Tour 3, Part I, Stop 3), the monarch decided to build a more enclosed square where bankers and merchants could discreetly conduct their work. In 1607, Henri IV appropriated two small islands located off the Ile de la Cité and joined them to the larger island. He then designed a triangular square surrounded by 32 houses of brick and stone and named it after the Dauphin, Louis XIII. Alas, the beautiful symmetry of the enclosed square was destroyed in 1874 when the houses on the eastern end were destroyed to give a better view of the Palais de Justice. A later designer realized that the vacuous facade was best hidden and had a curtain of trees planted on the east side in an attempt to restore the sense of a private square. **No. 14** boasts one of the few facades retaining its original look.

Pass between the buildings at the point of the triangle and you'll come to:

15. **Pont Neuf,** where it used to be said that at any hour of the day you could meet "a monk, a loose woman, and a white horse." Pont Neuf is Paris's oldest bridge (even though its name means "new bridge"). Henri III laid the first stone on May 31, 1578, yet was long gone by the time it was finished and officially opened by Henri IV 29 years later. Pont Neuf was the first stone bridge built that wasn't lined with houses. With a total of 12 arches, pont Neuf is actually two bridges (they don't quite line up)— one stretching from the Right Bank to the Ile de la Cité, the other stretching from the Left Bank to the island. Originally the bridge served as a lively social center where

Parisians went to do their banking, be entertained by jokers and street performers, and even have their teeth pulled.

Note the **statue of Henri IV,** erected by Louis XVIII using bronze melted down from a statue of Napoléon that once stood atop the column in place Vendôme.

Take a Break At 13 place du pont-Neuf is the **Café Henri IV,** an old-fashioned wine bar redolent with the aromas of freshly baked pies and strong cheeses. Try an open-face sandwich slathered with rich pâté, and wash it down with one of the excellent wines sold by the glass.

When you leave the cafe, walk down the stairs behind the statue of Henri IV into:

16. **Square du Vert-Galant,** created at about the same time as place Dauphine. This is about as close to the river as you can get without actually being in it; the square is at the level of the Ile de la Cité during the Gallo-Roman period, about 7m (23 ft.) lower than it is now. Enjoy the view of the Louvre and the gargoyles on pont Neuf. The shrubs, flower beds, and benches make this a great picnic spot. You can pick up drinks and snacks next to the park at the embarkation point for the tourist boats (*vedettes*) that ply the Seine.

To find the Métro, return to pont Neuf and turn left. Cross the bridge to the Right Bank and you'll reach the pont Neuf Métro station on your left.

The Latin Quarter

PART I   THE NORTHERN LATIN QUARTER

Start: Place St-Michel (Métro: St-Michel).

Finish: La Sorbonne.

Time: 3 to 5 hours.

Best Time: Any time during the day.

Worst Time: Tuesday, when the Musée National du Moyen Age is closed.

The Latin Quarter has been a place for independent spirits ever since the 12th century, when freethinking Pierre Abélard was driven from the school of Notre-Dame for challenging church teachings. The popular teacher took 3,000 students with him to the Left Bank and was soon followed by other brilliant teachers. Word spread throughout Europe about the intellectual storm in Paris, and students began streaming in; their common language was

Latin, and the village that grew up around them became known as the Latin Quarter.

For the last 800 years, the Latin Quarter has been Paris's educational center. A huge portion of the neighborhood south of rue des Ecoles is taken over by the Université de Paris, with its headquarters at the Sorbonne. Students drink, shop, carouse, and occasionally riot in the same maze of medieval streets where their predecessors did, though many of the streets near the Seine have become much more chic and today teem with tourists. You'll still find a certain bohemian flavor in the tiny restaurants and smoky bistros around montagne Ste-Geneviève and rue Mouffetard (see Part II), however, where struggling students can eat and drink relatively cheaply.

The Latin Quarter was the first Parisian neighborhood to emerge after the settlement of the Ile de la Cité. Because the Right Bank was too marshy to inhabit, a Gallo-Roman residential district developed on the Left Bank in the 2nd century. The land was cultivated with vineyards; stone for the new buildings was quarried from the area around the Jardin des Plantes. A road was built, now called rue St-Jacques, to link Lutèce with another Roman stronghold at Lyon. Two perpendicular roads followed the path of today's rue Soufflot and rue des Ecoles. At important intersections, archaeologists have even found remnants of baths, now housed in the Musée National du Moyen Age and the amphitheater at the Arènes de Lutèce.

With the 3rd-century Norman invasions, the Left Bank was virtually abandoned for the safety of the Ile de la Cité. Activity didn't pick up again until the 12th century, with the establishment of the influential Ste-Geneviève and St-Victor abbeys. Following Abélard's example, teachers impatient with the school of Notre-Dame held classes on street corners and at intersections. In the 13th century, these diverse study groups were organized into an association, L'Universitas, and placed under the pope's jurisdiction. In 1253, Robert de Sorbon, confessor of St. Louis, got permission to use three buildings as a theology school, and the Sorbonne was born. The Latin Quarter's ecclesiastical power center was completely independent from royal rule to the extent that it even sided with the English during the Hundred Years' War, recognizing Henry V of England as king.

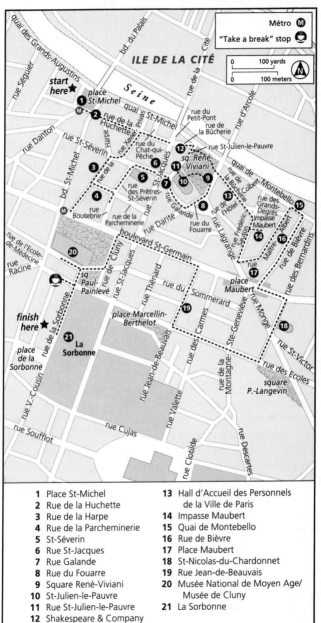

1 Place St-Michel	**13** Hall d'Accueil des Personnels
2 Rue de la Huchette	de la Ville de Paris
3 Rue de la Harpe	**14** Impasse Maubert
4 Rue de la Parcheminerie	**15** Quai de Montebello
5 St-Séverin	**16** Rue de Bièvre
6 Rue St-Jacques	**17** Place Maubert
7 Rue Galande	**18** St-Nicolas-du-Chardonnet
8 Rue du Fouarre	**19** Rue Jean-de-Beauvais
9 Square René-Viviani	**20** Musée National de Moyen Age/
10 St-Julien-le-Pauvre	Musée de Cluny
11 Rue St-Julien-le-Pauvre	**21** La Sorbonne
12 Shakespeare & Company	

To serve the growing population in the quarter, merchants filled the surrounding streets and alleys with shops. Scholars bought their roasted meat on rue de la Huchette, their parchment on rue de la Parcheminerie, and anything else they needed on rue Galande. Humble parish churches were enlarged to accommodate the growing population. St-Severin, St-Julien-le-Pauvre, and St-Etienne were constructed according to the new principles of Gothic architecture.

When the printing press was introduced to Paris in the 15th century, the scholarly Latin Quarter became the place of choice for printing shops. Rue St-Jacques was filled with printers and bookstores, perpetuating the intellectual tradition of the neighborhood. In the 17th and 18th centuries, members of an emerging bourgeoisie built houses here; their elaborate facades and carved doors make an interesting contrast with the simpler dwellings you'll see on this walk.

The revolution suppressed the university, but it was reborn as a secular institution under Napoléon in 1806. The Latin Quarter became a *quartier populaire* (common neighborhood), a place where students and artists starved, picturesquely, in garrets. This image was vividly incarnated in Henri Burger's novel *Scènes de la Vie de Bohème,* later the inspiration for the opera *La Bohème* and the Broadway musical *Rent.*

This tour begins and ends in the 19th-century Latin Quarter, but along the way you'll follow in the footsteps of the ancient Romans, whose roads defined the early neighborhood. You'll explore the web of streets around the St-Julien-le-Pauvre and St-Severin churches; they recall the life of medieval scholars and trace the later development of the neighborhood in the fine facades of 16th-, 17th-, and 18th-century houses. Don't be discouraged by the crush of visitors along rue de la Huchette and rue de la Harpe. Venture on and you'll have some fine medieval streets nearly to yourself.

• • • • • • • • • • • • • • •

Begin your tour at:

1. **Place St-Michel,** planned by Napoléon III and famous for its fountain, Davioud's 1860 sculpture of St. Michel slaying a dragon. To commemorate a modern form of dragon slaying, the names of those who died here fighting

the Nazis in 1944 are engraved on plaques around the square. Celebrating students from the Ecole des Beaux-Arts traditionally go for a swim in the fountain after their annual ball. Day and night, weekday and holiday, the intersection around the fountain buzzes with activity. Le Départ cafe is open 24 hours, the bookstores and fast-food outlets are usually jammed with students, and tourists hunt for postcards and souvenirs in the corner stalls.

Pass between the yellow awnings of **Gibert Jeune** (one of the Latin Quarter's few remaining truly collegiate bookstores) and turn onto:

2. **Rue de la Huchette,** a pedestrian alley whose name hasn't changed in 800 years. It has always been a busy commercial street, though the activity has shifted from cutting gems and roasting meat to making souvlakia and couscous. Most of the houses were built in the 18th century, and if you can keep your eyes trained above the Greek restaurants that monopolize the street level, it's not hard to find traces of the old shops.

At **no. 28** (on your left) is the **Hôtel Mont-Blanc,** former residence of American author Eliot Harold Paul (1891–1958), whose *Last Time I Saw Paris* (1942) chronicled the city in the 1920s and 1930s. As you walk, on your left you'll pass **rue du Chat-qui-Pêche** ("Street of the Fishing Cat"). There's nothing to see here, but it does happen to be Paris's narrowest street. Before the quay was built, the Seine sometimes rose above its banks, flooding the cellars of the houses here. Legend has it that an enterprising cat took advantage of its good fortune and went fishing in the cellars—hence the street's name.

At **no. 23** is the **Théâtre de la Huchette,** which has been playing the same two plays by Eugene Ionesco, *The Bald Soprano* and *The Lesson,* since 1957. At **no. 14** notice the letter Y in relief on the building's facade. In the 15th century, a popular store sold a crucial undergarment called a *lie-gregue,* which fastened a man's breeches to his socks. Its logo Y was a pun on the French letter *y,* which is pronounced *i grec.* The logo is also visible in the ironwork. Push the buzzer at **no. 11** and take a peek at the 17th-century wooden staircase inside. The young Napoléon

Bonaparte lived at **no. 10** for a while in 1795 before he began his meteoric rise to power. He paid 3F (.45€ or 55¢) a week for his room. Notice the sign A LA HURE D'OR (The Golden Boar's Head) still on the facade of **no. 4,** built in 1729.

Retracing your steps, turn left on 13th-century rue Xavier-Privas; go right on rue St-Séverin and then left on:

3. **Rue de la Harpe,** an ancient Roman road that linked the baths under the Musée de Cluny with the residences on the slopes of montagne St-Geneviève (site of the Panthéon). Until its northern end was absorbed by the construction of boulevard St-Michel in 1855, this was an important Left Bank artery, which explains the presence of several upper-crust mansions. All the old houses on the left—**nos. 23, 27, 29, 51,** and **53**—date from the 17th century. **No. 35** is an 18th-century mansion with an imposing portal topped by sculpted masks. **No. 45** is another 18th-century mansion, notable for its masks and ironwork.

Double back and make a right on:

4. **Rue de la Parcheminerie.** Though relatively subdued now, this street once provided a link between the important rue de la Harpe and rue St-Jacques, and teemed with professional letter writers, booksellers, copyists, and parchment sellers. Now the **Abbey Bookshop,** at **no. 29,** specializing in Canadian titles, carries on the intellectual tradition in a mid-18th-century building with an elegant iron balcony and a sculpted bas-relief.

Continue to the corner of **rue Boutebrie** on your right and the **courtyard garden** (a former burial ground) of the church of St-Séverin on your left. You might want to take a look at the 16th-century buildings at **nos. 6, 8,** and **10** before heading to the corner garden. Although the garden is open only on Sundays between 10am and 12:30pm, you can look inside the gate at the galleries of the medieval charnel house that once stood here.

Now go in the main door of:

5. **St-Séverin,** off rue des Prêtres-St-Séverin. The original building, an oratory, was built to honor a hermit named Séverin, who lived here in the 6th century. Norsemen

burned it down in the 11th century, and a new chapel was erected in its place. By the end of the 11th century, it had become the Left Bank's parish church. The flamboyant Gothic building you see today was begun in the early 13th century, and the work continued well into the 16th century.

The two ambulatories (one currently filled with chairs) are what really make St-Séverin unique among Paris churches. Sadly, the organ obscures your view of the rose window, but note that the organ case was built by Dupré. Saint-Saëns is said to have played on it.

The rest of the stained glass behind the altar looks like an Impressionist painting, with great swaths of color. Best viewed at a distance, the windows—designed by Jean Bazaine in 1966—depict the Seven Sacraments. Since you're not expected to know what the rites are by just looking at them, a small plaque underneath each window explains what each represents. The chapel to the right of the altar (Chapelle de la Communion) contains some beautiful Georges Roualt etchings done between 1922 and 1927 and pulled by Jacquenin, a master Parisian printer. There's a biography of Roualt on the door to the left of the chapel. This room also holds an extraordinary G. Schneider rendition of the crucifixion (1989).

Leave by the side door on **rue St-Séverin** and turn right. You'll pass a strangely narrow house at **no. 12,** containing only two windows on each floor, before reaching:

6. **Rue St-Jacques,** probably the first street in Paris, built by the Romans to link Lutèce with the city of Orléans in the south. Many vestiges of the Gallo-Roman era have been found along rue St-Jacques, including the baths at the Musée de Cluny, the forum at rue Soufflot, an aqueduct near rue Guy-Lussac, and a necropolis near boulevard Port-Royal. Still a major axis, the road crosses the Ile de la Cité at Petit Pont and becomes rue St-Martin on the Left Bank. Two paving stones from the road were recovered and placed near the door of St-Julien-le-Pauvre church.

Cross rue St-Jacques onto:

7. **Rue Galande,** which was the beginning of the Roman road leading to Lyon. In the 12th century, it was a

bustling commercial street; in the 17th century it became a residential district for prosperous clergymen and military officers before descending into genteel seediness in the 18th. As in most of the Latin Quarter, the solidity and fine architectural details of the old houses have once again attracted upscale residents.

The **Caveau des Oubliettes** cabaret, at **no. 52,** dates from the 17th century, though the faux medieval half-timber walls were added in the 19th. The cellar had been a nightclub for centuries and is now used as a museum of torture devices (only for patrons of the upstairs cabaret). The massive portal and sculpted facade of **no. 65** reflect the prestige of the aristocratic families that inhabited it from the 16th to the 18th century. The exotic store **Le Chat Huant,** at **no. 50,** is a medieval house that was restored in the 17th century. Try to get into **no. 46,** the **Auberge aux Deux Signes** restaurant, to see the vaulted cellars of St-Blaise, a 13th-century church that once stood here.

At **no. 42** is **Studio Galande,** currently a cinema famous for its weekend midnight showings of *The Rocky Horror Picture Show.* Notice the 14th-century bas-relief of St. Julien le Hospitalier in his boat. According to legend, Julien was deep in remorse after having accidentally killed his parents. He decided to build a hospital for poor people as penance. One day, Julien and his wife gave a leper a ride across the Seine; the leper turned out to be Christ, and Julien was pardoned. The bas-relief most likely came from the church of St-Julien-le-Pauvre. **Nos. 29** and **31** probably were built in the 16th century, though the splendidly carved wood gable dates from the end of the Gothic period in the 15th century.

Now make a left onto:

8. **Rue du Fouarre,** popularly known as rue Trou-Punais (stink-hole) in medieval times. Nevertheless, open-air classes began on the street in the 12th century with the arrival of Abélard and other teachers from the Notre-Dame school. In the spirit of humility and self-abnegation, students were required to sit on the ground before their professors. They began placing bundles of straw *(fouarres)* under themselves, and the street took on its new name. Dante was supposed to have been one of the straw-sitters

in 1304, around the time the street was acquiring a reputation for ribaldry and shenanigans that prompted Charles V to barricade it in 1358.

Little medieval flavor remains, but notice the eccentric 18th-century building at **no. 8** before turning left onto the:

9. **Square René-Viviani,** a shady little park graced with lime trees, lilac bushes, and a false acacia planted in 1601—the oldest tree in Paris. The square offers a superb view of Notre-Dame cathedral; its proportions contrast strikingly with the comparatively minuscule church of:

10. **St-Julien-le-Pauvre,** on the south side of the square. In the 6th century, when the first chapel was built here, the spot was at the busiest intersection in Paris—the corner of rue St-Jacques leading to Orléans and rue Galande leading to Lyon. The original chapel was destroyed by the Normans in the 9th century, and it wasn't until the 12th century that work began on the current church. It was finished at about the same time as Notre-Dame and, like its big sister across the Seine, marks a transition from Romanesque to Gothic architecture. For several centuries it was the church of choice for the teachers and students of the University, especially participants in the classes on rue du Fouarre. After a 16th-century student riot seriously damaged the interior, the church fell into disuse. The facade was renovated in the 17th century and the church fully restored in the 19th, when it was given to the Greek Orthodox Church. To the right of the entrance are a medieval iron wellhead and two paving stones from the Roman road to Orléans. Inside, the beautiful chancel is enclosed by a wooden screen hung with icons.

When you come out of the church, go right on:

11. **Rue St-Julien-le-Pauvre** and keep an eye out for **no. 14** (on your left), the mansion of Isaac de Laffemas, governor of the Petit Châtelet prison. It has a wonderful portal dating from the late 17th century. **Nos. 4, 6,** and **10** were built in the 17th and 18th centuries on medieval foundations.

Go left at the corner of rue St-Julien-le-Pauvre onto **rue de la Bûcherie,** named after the logs *(bûches)* that used to arrive here by boat for distribution in Paris. This part of the street is a peaceful niche of benches and trees running next to the busy quay. At **no. 37** you'll find:

12. **Shakespeare and Company,** whose outdoor bulletin board is usually covered with notices from starving writers begging for work or trying to sell their old shoes. Not Sylvia Beach's original, this bookstore is run by George Bates Whitman (self-professed grandson of Walt). Whitman purchased part of Sylvia Beach's library, which is housed at the top of a treacherous flight of stairs. You're welcome to browse through Beach's personal collection. Each book you purchase here will be stamped with the official inscription: SHAKESPEARE AND CO., KILOMÈTRE ZÉRO, PARIS. It's open daily noon to midnight.

Next door at **no. 39** is one of the smallest houses in Paris. Built in the beginning of the 16th century, it looks like the gingerbread house in the Hansel and Gretel story. It's now Le Petit Châtelet restaurant.

Cross the square René-Viviani and pick up rue de la Bûcherie again. The most interesting building on this street is at **nos. 13–15,** the:

13. **Hall d'Accueil des Personnels de la Ville de Paris (Paris Administration School),** at the corner of rue de la Bûcherie and rue de l'Hôtel-Colbert. It's on the 15th-century site of the first medical school in Paris, though most of what you see was built in the 17th and 18th centuries.

Continue on rue de la Bûcherie to rue Fréderic-Sauton. You'll find yourself on one of those enchanting squares that makes exploring old Paris such a delight. Turn right and you'll see:

14. **Impasse Maubert** immediately on your left. In 1206, the patriarch of Constantinople created Paris's first college here in an attempt to unite the Greek and Latin churches. Many of the doors along this 13th-century cobblestone alley hide long passages leading to yards surrounded by a tangle of even more ramshackle structures.

Continue along rue Fréderic-Sauton and make a sharp left on rue Lagrange onto **rue Maître-Albert,** named after Albert, a medieval professor who taught here. Most of the houses on this street date from the 17th century and are linked by a network of subterranean passages to buildings on rue Fréderic-Sauton and Impasse Maubert.

You'll soon arrive at:

15. **Quai de Montebello,** the calmest and most scenic quay on the Seine. You may wish to browse the stalls of the *bouquinistes* (booksellers) who have been selling volumes along here for almost 400 years. The first *bouquinistes* hawked their wares on foot, walking through the streets carrying their books in willow baskets suspended by straps around their necks. In 1578, at the beginning of Henri III's reign, they were ordered to find permanent places from which to sell their goods, and about 25 years later they set up shop on the quays.

Turn right on quai de Montebello and right again on:

16. **Rue de Bièvre.** It's hard to imagine that this street of 17th- and 18th-century town houses was a canal until the turn of the 20th century. La Bièvre was a river that brought water from its source, near Versailles, through south Paris, where it was canalized to empty into the Seine. The tanneries, dye works, mills, and textile plants along its banks dumped so much waste into the river and its canals that it eventually became a health hazard and had to be paved over. Rumor has it that Dante lived on this street-canal in the late 13th or early 14th century and began writing the *Divine Comedy.* A more recent illustrious resident was the late French president François Mitterrand, who lived at **no. 22.** During his presidency, Mitterrand insisted on residing in his private home rather than in the Palais de l'Elysée, the traditional home for France's presidents. At **no. 20** a secluded **garden** is perfect for a romantic summer picnic surrounded by roses.

At the end of rue de Bièvre you'll find yourself on:

17. **Place Maubert.** Like rue du Fouarre, this square was an open-air classroom in the 12th century, before the students and teachers headed off to the colleges on Ste-Geneviève hill. Later it became a notorious execution site nicknamed Maubert Cesspit. People were hung, pilloried, burned, and put to the rack for heresy, blasphemy, and other crimes. So many Huguenots were killed here that it

became a place of pilgrimage. Not a trace of the square's grisly history remained after Baron Haussmann's 19th-century renovations, but you can see a popular outdoor **food market** (open Tues, Thurs, and Sat mornings) and some interesting **old houses** at the corner of rue Maître-Albert.

Follow the direction of traffic on boulevard St-Germain and make a right on rue des Bernardins, where you'll see on your left the church of:

18. **St-Nicolas-du-Chardonnet.** This site was once a field of thistles (*chardons*), and the original place of worship was a 13th-century chapel dedicated to St. Nicolas, the patron saint of boatmen. Construction of the present church began in 1656, though the facade was finished only in 1934. The most striking external features are the carved wooden doors on the rue des Bernardins side. They were designed by Charles Le Brun, the 17th-century classical painter who was a great favorite of Louis XIV.

St-Nicolas-du-Chardonnet was fortunate to have Le Brun as a parishioner, since he contributed a great deal to the church. Once you get inside, turn to the right to view his *Martyrdom of John the Baptist.* In the first chapel on the left wall as you enter is Corot's *Baptism of Christ.* Continue around behind the altar, and as you come to the other side you'll see the tomb of Le Brun's mother as well as an Antoine Coysevox memorial to Le Brun and his wife. Above the altar and on the ceiling are more fine paintings by Le Brun. This church is one of the few that still holds mass in Latin.

Continue on rue des Bernardins, cross rue Monge, and make a right on rue des Ecoles. (Across the street is the **square Paul-Langevin,** another good spot for a picnic.) Take a right onto:

19. **Rue Jean-de-Beauvais,** created in the 14th century and once filled with printing shops. Go down the stairs on the right behind the statue of Romanian poet Mihail Eminescu to **no. 9 bis,** one of the Sorbonne's first college chapels, built in 1375 by Raymond du Temple, who also worked on the Louvre. Its Gothic spire is the only one of its period left in the city. Since 1882 it has been used as a Romanian Orthodox church.

Continue to boulevard St-Germain, make a left, and walk to rue de Cluny. Make a left and proceed to square Paul-Painlevé and you'll see the entrance to the:

20. **Musée National du Moyen Age/Thermes de Cluny,** of outstanding architectural and historical interest. Around the beginning of the 3rd century, the wealthy guild of Paris boatmen built a complex of Roman baths here. Its life as a bath center was a short one, since the barbarians came less than a century later and burned it to the ground. Nevertheless, important vestiges remain in the museum, including the relatively well-preserved frigidarium.

About 1,000 years later, the property was purchased by Pierre of Chalûs, abbé de Cluny, as a residence for visiting abbots. "Wherever the wind blows, the abbey of Cluny holds riches" was once a local saying. The wealth and prestige of this medieval order is evident in the ornamentation of the main courtyard on place Paul-Painlevé, which contains friezes, gargoyles, dormers, and decorative turrets. Most of the mansion dates from the 15th century, when it was rebuilt by Jacques d'Amboise, but the 14th-century facade is visible on the boulevard St-Germain side.

Inside the museum is one of the world's greatest collections of medieval art and artifacts, including jewelry, stained-glass windows, and the splendid Unicorn Tapestries, as well as the original Abbot's Chapel. Even if you save the museum visit for another time, make sure to take in that Flamboyant Gothic courtyard. The museum is open Wednesday to Monday 9:15am to 5:45pm, and there's an admission fee.

When you leave, take rue de la Sorbonne from square Paul-Painlevé. Turn right on rue des Ecoles.

Take a Break At **no. 49** is the **Brasserie Balzar,** a bustling, fashionable place with very good food. It has hosted many of France's most famous intellectuals, including the likes of Jean-Paul Sartre, and it's always full, even at odd hours. In fact, one of the brasserie's chief attractions is that it serves full meals at all hours.

Leaving the brasserie, take rue des Ecoles to the right and make a right onto rue de la Sorbonne. Continue until you reach:

21. **La Sorbonne.** Though the 19th-century architecture seems rather severe, the Sorbonne has exerted a powerful influence on the Latin Quarter's intellectual life for nearly 800 years. In 1253, Robert de Sorbon, St. Louis's confessor, founded the Sorbonne (with the help of the king) for poor students who wished to pursue theological studies. He wanted it to be a place where they could live and go to school without having to worry about money. The Sorbonne soon became France's center of theological study and attracted such famous teachers as St. Thomas Aquinas and Roger Bacon and such famous students as Dante, Calvin, and Longfellow. In 1469, France's first printing press was set up here. During the Nazi occupation, the Sorbonne became the headquarters for the Resistance, and the unrest of May 1968 centered around the Sorbonne as striking students barricaded streets and battled the police. Since the 1968 protests, the university departments have decentralized, though the Sorbonne remains the headquarters of the system.

The courtyard and galleries are open to the public when the university is in session, and in the Cour d'Honneur are statues of Victor Hugo and Louis Pasteur. Opposite the statues, a large colorful mural by Weertz depicts a 15th-century festival.

This ends Part I of the Latin Quarter tour. If you don't want to continue with Part II, make a right at place de la Sorbonne and a right on boulevard St-Michel at the other end of the square. You'll reach the Cluny–La Sorbonne Métro station. If you do wish to continue, Part II begins where the first part ended, at the Sorbonne.

PART II   THE SOUTHERN LATIN QUARTER

Start: La Sorbonne (Métro: Cluny–La Sorbonne).

Finish: Mosquée de Paris and Institut Musulman.

Time: About 3 hours.

Best Time: Mornings from Tuesday to Sunday, so you can visit the Mouffetard market while it's open.

Worst Time: Mondays and afternoons, when the market is closed.

P art II of this tour begins with the scholar's Latin Quarter and takes you up to the montagne Ste-Geneviève, inspired by devotion to Ste. Geneviève. The influential Ste-Geneviève abbey sparked the urbanization of this neighborhood in the 12th and 13th centuries, a process that continued with the establishment of numerous colleges in the area. Though the abbey no longer stands, Ste-Geneviève is venerated in both the marvelous St-Etienne-du-Mont church and the Panthéon, which was built in the saint's honor.

You'll then go down the south side of montagne Ste-Geneviève on scenic rue Mouffetard. The steep, winding streets that lead down to the St-Médard church seem part of a country village in the heart of Paris. As early as the 9th century, local residents were planting vineyards and cultivating fields here. Later, the village's location along rue Mouffetard (on the Roman road to Lyon) and near the Biévre river favored the growth of trade. Though the neighborhood was affiliated with the nearby Ste-Geneviève abbey, it didn't officially become a part of Paris until 1724. The houses date from the 16th to the 18th century, but the casual, unpretentious spirit of the neighborhood owes much of its character to the working-class cabarets and clubs that sprang up in the 19th century. Despite some restoration and renovation in the last 30 years, this colorful area remains remarkably intact.

● ● ● ● ● ● ● ● ● ● ● ● ● ● ● ●

Exit the Sorbonne (see Part I for details), turn left, walk to place de la Sorbonne, and stay on the right side of the square. Turn right at rue Champollion, a narrow 18th-century street of student cafes and art-house cinemas. (The street is named after an Egyptologist member of the College.) Make a right on rue des Ecoles. You'll pass the square Paul-Painlevé and then come to the:

1. **Collège de France.** Rebelling against the narrow-mindedness of the teachings of the Sorbonne, François I founded the college in 1530. The professors at the new Collège de France were paid by the king rather than the students, a radical change from the Sorbonne's procedure. The school began as a trilingual institution, teaching Latin,

Greek, and Hebrew—another departure. Not long after its founding, courses in mathematics, philosophy, surgery, medicine, law, Arabic, and astronomy were also made available; while Louis XV was king, a French literature course was added, the first of its kind. Reflecting a tradition of nondiscriminatory policies, the inscription outside the school reads DOCET OMNIA ("All are taught here").

Turn right on rue Jean-de-Beauvais and walk to the intersection of:

2. **Rue de Lanneau and Impasse Chartière.** A complex of Gallo-Roman baths was discovered on this picturesque corner. Impasse Chartière had been the site of the 15th-century Collège de Coqueret, considered the birthplace of the French language: In the 16th century, a group of students here promulgated the novel idea that the French language was as rich and sophisticated as Latin or Greek, the two languages that every educated person was already expected to know.

   The ivied building at **no. 11** rue de Lanneau has been welcoming guests since 1627. Now it's a restaurant, **Le Coupe Chou.** Opened in 1185, this quiet street of 16th- and 17th-century houses had been filled with bookstores and printing shops serving the nearby colleges. Make a left on rue de Lanneau and take a look at **rue d'Ecosse** on the right, named for the Scottish students who lived here until the 17th century.

3. **Rue de la Montagne-Ste-Geneviève,** is another ancient street that had been part of the Roman road linking Lutèce to Lyon. In the Middle Ages, the road was the main route to the Ste-Geneviève abbey on top of the hill (see below).

   Straight ahead is the former entrance to the:

4. **Ecole Polytechnique,** France's most prestigious institute of higher learning, now located on the outskirts of Paris. Its illustrious alumni include numerous government ministers, as well as former French president Valéry Giscard d'Estaing.

   Behind the stylized facades on rue de la Montagne-Ste-Geneviève lie twisting networks of:

The Southern Latin Quarter

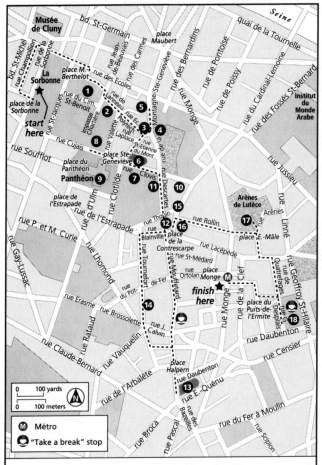

1 Collège de France

2 Rue de Lanneau and Impasse Chartière

3 Rue de la Montagne-Ste-Geneviève

4 Ecole Polytechnique

5 Passages and courtyards

6 St-Etienne-du-Mont

7 Lycée Henri IV

8 Bibliothèque Ste-Geneviève

9 Panthéon

10 Paris's wall

11 Rue Descartes

12 Rue Mouffetard

13 St-Médard

14 Rue Tournefort

15 Rue du Cardinal-Lemoine

16 Rue Rollin

17 Arènes de Lutèce

18 Mosquée de Paris and Institut Musulman

5. **Passages and courtyards.** Take a behind-the-scenes look at the neighborhood by turning left and going downhill on rue de la Montagne-Ste-Geneviève. Press the button at **no. 34** to enter a series of courtyards filled with plants and trees. This was the site of an 18th-century religious college, and now you'll see students on their way to and from classes in one of the martial-arts schools that occupy this appealing ensemble of buildings. On the left is a building with a wide staircase. Go up the stairs; on the first floor, you'll come to a small wooden door that leads onto a cul-de-sac known as Cour-des-Boeufs. Return to the street, turn right on rue de la Montagne-Ste-Geneviève, and continue climbing the Ste-Geneviève "mountain." Notice the 17th-century building at **no. 47** and the 16th-century building at **no. 51** that had been a cabaret. You'll soon come to the church of:

6. **St-Etienne-du-Mont,** a unique and thoroughly enchanting blend of late Gothic and Renaissance styles. Construction began late in the 15th century to replace a previous church that had become too small for the burgeoning neighborhood population. Completed and consecrated in the 17th century, the church holds a shrine to Ste. Geneviève as well as the remains of Pascal and Racine. The lovely 17th-century rood screen is the only one left in Paris, and on either side staircases spiral to the top. The epitaphs of Pascal and Racine are on the right, followed by the shrine of Ste. Geneviève. Although the saint's relics were burned during the revolution, her sarcophagus stone was later found in the abbey of Ste-Geneviève (see below) and is now encased in this copper shrine. Continuing your way around, you'll see the tombs of Pascal and Racine behind the chancel as well as stained-glass windows, some from the 16th and 17th centuries.

When you leave the church, you'll note that directly opposite it across rue Clovis is the:

7. **Lycée Henri IV.** One of the city's best-known high schools, the Lycée Henri IV is housed on the historic site of the Ste-Geneviève abbey. Early in the 6th century, Clovis, king of the Franks, and his wife, Clotilde, built a basilica in which they and Ste. Geneviève were eventually buried. The basilica was destroyed by the Norman invasions, but a new

church was erected in the 12th century, and it became a rich and powerful abbey. A village developed around the abbey and its vineyards. The abbey was torn apart in the revolution, and since then, the few remaining structures have been occupied by the high school. The 12th-century Clovis Tower is still standing, as are the remains of the refectory, kitchens, and Gothic cellars, but they're not open to visitors.

Continue along rue Clovis, crossing place Ste-Geneviève, which is on your right as you face the lycée. Cross rue Valette and you'll see the entrance to the:

8. **Bibliothèque Ste-Geneviève,** on the right. The library was created in 1624 to house the priceless books and manuscripts of the Ste-Geneviève abbey and is the sole monastic library to survive the revolution. Completed in 1850, the current building is a masterpiece of steel architecture and contains 2,700,000 volumes, including manuscripts of Baudelaire, Verlaine, Rimbaud, Gide, and countless others. In addition to the books, the library boasts sculpture by Coysevox and Houdon as well as Gobelins tapestries. Bring a passport, fill out a form identifying yourself as a researcher, and you can tour the immense library, which is open Monday to Friday 10am to 10pm (Sat until 5pm).

Across the street from the library is the:

9. **Panthéon,** the most magnificent of the monuments inspired by Ste-Geneviève. In 1744, Louis XV fell seriously ill. He vowed that if he recovered he'd rebuild the Ste-Geneviève abbey in the patron saint's honor. On recovering, he entrusted the job to the marquis de Marigny, Mme de Pompadour's brother, who passed on the responsibility to architect Jacques-Germain Soufflot. Soufflot admired the classical monuments of northern Italy and medieval architecture. In the Panthéon he intended to combine "the lightness of Gothic structures with the purity of Greek architecture." The original plans called for a church centered on a shrine to the saint, but construction stopped due to financial difficulties and Soufflot's death. After the death of an important revolution-era politician by the name of Mirabeau, the French parliament decided that the Ste-Geneviève church should be changed into a "Temple of Fame" to hold the remains

of all the great men of France, the first of whom would be Mirabeau.

Shortly after Mirabeau's burial, Voltaire's remains were exhumed and moved to the Panthéon, which became a "temple dedicated to all the gods." Among its denizens are Jean-Jacques Rousseau, Victor Hugo, Paul Painlevé, Louis Braille (inventor of the reading system for the blind), Emile Zola, and Jean Moulin (a Resistance fighter tortured to death by the Nazis). Certain "gods" became decidedly less godlike as political winds changed, and the remains of overzealous revolutionaries Mirabeau and Marat were transferred elsewhere. Recent additions have been Pierre and Marie Curie (the "first lady so honored in our history for her own merits," according to the late François Mitterrand) and writer/activist André Malraux.

Before entering the crypt, notice the striking frescoes, *Scenes from St. Geneviève's Life* on the right wall and *St. Geneviève Watching over Paris and Bringing Food to the City* on the left wall. Both are by Puvis de Chavannes. The Panthéon is open daily: April to September 9:30am to 6:30pm and October to March 10am to 6:15pm; there's an admission fee.

Head back toward St-Etienne-du-Mont along rue Clovis. Continue to **no. 3,** where you'll see a hunk of:

10. **Paris's wall.** This was part of Philippe-Auguste's 10m-high (33-ft.) wall marking the limit of 13th-century Paris. Before leaving for his third Crusade, Philippe-Auguste decided to protect the population of Paris from invasion by building a sturdy wall. Construction began in 1190 on the Right Bank and continued onto the Left Bank, where it was completed in 1213. The wall was used for about 150 years before Charles V replaced it in the 14th century.

Retrace your steps and make a left onto:

11. **Rue Descartes,** a lively street of cheap restaurants and sidewalk cafes. Formerly called rue Bordelles, it was part of the Gallo-Roman road to Lyon that connected rue de la Montagne-Ste-Geneviève (see above) with rue Mouffetard (see below), outside the 13th-century wall. At **no. 39** is the house where French poet Paul Verlaine (1844–96) died. The 1869 publication of *Fêtes galantes* made him a major figure in the bohemian literary world,

but he spent his later life in a haze of absinthe, his "green muse." A plaque on **no. 50,** below the third floor, marks the site of the Bordelles gate in the Philippe-Auguste wall.

Continue on rue Descartes until it turns into:

12. **Rue Mouffetard,** which has become famous for the hordes of tourists packing its colorful outdoor **food market** that's open Tuesday to Sunday 7am to 1pm. Nevertheless, "La Mouffe" and its side streets retain a strong flavor of their origins as a 16th-century village. Most of the buildings are at least partly original, though many were redone in the 17th and 18th centuries.

No. 6 was a butcher shop in the 18th century, which you can surmise by looking at the two mammoth bulls in bas-relief on the facade. Although a recent restoration and a coat of bright gold paint make the bulls look brand new, the building dates from the 18th century.

Straight ahead on your left is **place de la Contrescarpe,** an animated square bordered by several large cafes. Located right outside the city gates, this intersection naturally became a favorite rendezvous of rowdies and merrymakers in the Middle Ages. Note the sign to your left across the square, *Cabaret de la Pomme De Pin,* recalling the 16th-century cabaret that was a favorite haunt of Rabelais.

Continue down the winding rue Mouffetard. **No. 53** doesn't look like much from the outside, but when the building was being demolished in 1938, a treasure trove of 18th-century gold coins was discovered, placed there by Louis Nivelle, advisor to Louis XV. Worth about 25 million francs (3.8 million euros/10 million dollars), the booty was distributed among Nivelle's heirs, the city of Paris, and the lucky workers who discovered it.

At the corner of **rue du Pot-de-Fer** is a **fountain.** Although the spigot looks insignificant, it was installed by Marie de Médici in 1624 as part of her plan to bring water from outside Paris to her Palais du Luxembourg. The excess was intended to ameliorate Paris's chronic water shortages. (Until the revolution, Parisians had to make do with a quart of water a day per person.) On a stroll down this pedestrian lane, notice the gabled house on the corner next to the fountain and the 18th-century door at **no. 7.**

Return to rue Mouffetard. The orderly design and neat rows of windows at **no. 61** contrast starkly with the rest of the street. In 1656, a convent was built here, and it began to fall apart about 60 years later. The Mother Superior prevailed on the marquise de Maintenon to pay for its reconstruction, and the marquise entrusted the job to a local official. This gentleman fell in love with a pretty novice and helped plot her escape from the order. Alerted to the scheme, the Mother Superior immediately hid the girl, which threw the amorous builder into such a fury that he refused to proceed with the work. Caught between her duty to the novice and her fervent desire for a new building, the Mother Superior was forced to relent. The nun was released to the official, and the new building was erected. It later became a barracks.

Take a Break   At **no. 67, La Maison des Tartes** is a cozy cafe serving freshly baked savory and sweet tarts. Try the smoked salmon with spinach or the delectable lemon tart. Two doors down at **no. 69,** The **Maison du Vieux-Chêne** restaurant gets its name from the carving of an oak *(chêne)* on the facade, one of the few wooden building reliefs left in Paris. The restaurant had been a hotbed of revolutionary activity in 1848 and then a public dance hall. The pointed arch at **no. 81** marked the entrance to a 17th-century chapel.

Farther down the street, the old houses evoke village life even more. At **no. 122,** the brightly colored relief labeled A LA BONNE SOURCE, showing a boy and girl at a fountain, is particularly endearing. Note the 16th-century dormer at **no. 126** and the extravagantly painted facade at **no. 134** before turning left at the square in front of the church of:

13. **St-Médard.** The first church was probably built here in the 7th or 8th century at the intersection of rue Mouffetard and the Bièvre river (see Part I of this tour). Destroyed by the Normans, it was rebuilt in the 12th century as the parish church of a market village, a character it has retained despite renovations and extensions that began in the 15th century and ended at the turn of the 20th. In the 18th century, it became the scene of a strange collective hysteria when a Jansenist deacon was buried in the cemetery (now the front

square). His tomb acquired a reputation for miraculous healing at a time when the Jansenists were cruelly persecuted. An epidemic of trances, cures, and convulsions led Louis XV to close the cemetery and forbid any further miracles. BY ORDER OF THE KING, LET GOD NO MIRACLE PERFORM IN THIS PLACE read the sign on the cemetery gate.

The interior merits a look, especially for the 16th-century triptych behind the pulpit and the good selection of 17th- and 18th-century French religious paintings.

Leave the church by the side door to the left of the altar. Make a left on rue Daubenton and you'll come to rue Mouffetard. Turn right and head up the hill, where at **no. 104** you'll find the entry to the Passage des Postes. Take this narrow alley to rue Lhomonde and make a right. You'll come to an attractive square. Then take:

14. **Rue Tournefort** on the other side of the square to the right. This sedate street was the victim of a rather overly enthusiastic renewal program in the 1970s, but at **no. 20** (at the corner of rue du Pot-de-Fer) you'll notice the former street name RUE NEUVE-SAINTE-GENEVIÈVE engraved on the side of the building. Farther up on the left you'll cross **rue Amyot,** which, for reasons that haven't yet become clear, was long called rue du Puits-qui-Parle (Street of the Talking Wells).

Make a right on **rue Blainville,** admiring the gables and ironwork on the 17th- and 18th-century houses, and you'll arrive at place de la Contrescarpe. Head onto:

15. **Rue du Cardinal-Lemoine** on the other side of the square and you'll see Hemingway's first home in Paris on the left at **no. 74.** In his memoirs of those early years, *A Moveable Feast,* Hemingway wrote of the goatherd who used to stop before his building and the woman who would fill a pot with milk from one of the "heavy-bagged, black milk-goats" in the herd.

Turn right onto the pedestrian:

16. **Rue Rollin.** René Descartes (1596–1650) used to stay at **no. 14** during his trips to Paris, and Emile Zola (1840–1902) lived in **no. 4.** Go down the stairs at the end of the street and cross rue Monge to rue Navarre, where you'll find the entrance to the:

17. **Arènes de Lutèce,** a Roman amphitheater. Archaeologists believe that the amphitheater was built in the late 1st century, which makes it the oldest Parisian monument. With its 36 rows of stone seats, it had a seating capacity of 15,000. As the barbarians approached at the end of the 3rd century, terrified inhabitants of the Left Bank fled to the Ile de la Cité and used stones from the amphitheater to wall the island. By the 4th century, it was used as a cemetery. It was buried when a moat was dug around Philippe-Auguste's city wall in the late 12th century. Then in 1869 the amphitheater was rediscovered and restored, and today the Arènes de Lutèce is a public garden featuring the square Capitan, named for a sponsor of the restoration. You'll always find lots of children playing here, watched over by their nannies or parents; you might even find a full-fledged game of *boules* (similar to the Italian game, bocce) in progress.

    Exit the amphitheater from the same entrance and make a left on rue Lacépède and a right on rue de Quatrefages. Continue along to place du Puits-de-l'Ermite. On your left, at **no. 2,** will be the:

18. **Mosquée de Paris and Institut Musulman,** constructed between 1922 and 1926. As you enter these buildings, notice the grand patio with its cedar woodwork, eucalyptus plants, and gurgling fountain. On the walls of the mosque, some lovely mosaic friezes bear quotations from the Koran, and the prayer rooms house an incredible collection of hand-woven carpets, some from the 17th century. The Institut Musulman teaches Arabic and Islamic culture.

    Take a Break If you're hungry for lunch or just a snack, try the **Moorish cafe** or the **Middle Eastern restaurant** on the other side of the mosque at **no. 39 rue Geoffroy St-Hilaire.** The reasonable prices and Arabian Nights decor have made it a popular hangout for local students. Recommended are the delicious baklava and strong, sweet Turkish coffee.

    You can find the Place Monge Métro station from place du Puits-de-l'Ermite by turning right at rue Larrey and left at rue Dolomieu.

The Marais

PART I THE CENTRAL MARAIS

Start: Church of St-Paul–St-Louis (Métro: St-Paul).

Finish: Church of St-Paul–St-Louis.

Time: 3 to 5 hours.

Best Time: Weekdays when the courtyards of the hôtels are open.

Worst Time: Weekends and holidays, unless your interest is shopping in the boutiques along rue des Francs-Bourgeois, as they remain open on Sunday.

Few Paris neighborhoods have suffered as many reversals of fortune as the Marais. Beginning as swampland (*marais*), the district glittered with the arrival of royalty in the 14th century but then sank into abandonment and decay after the revolution. It was rediscovered in the 1960s and its mansions were repaired. Today, the Marais is back in fashion, thriving as a hub for Paris's gay life as well as literary, artistic, and entertainment figures whose taste for elegant shops and fine restaurants has restored the luster to the royal quarter.

Although a 4th-century basilica was erected on the site of St-Gervais–St-Protais, for many centuries the marshy land on the Right Bank seemed suitable for nothing but pastures and vegetable gardens. The Marais was only lightly inhabited until the 12th century, when the Knights Templar arrived. This exclusive military/religious order began in Jerusalem in 1128 to protect Crusaders and found that it paid off handsomely. Establishing their headquarters in the north Marais, they cultivated the land and built an enormous walled compound from which they ran their financial empire. By the 13th century, they owned most of the Marais. Other religious orders followed the Templars, and the Marais's wilds were slowly populated. In 1307, Philippe le Bel came to the unhappy realization that the Templars were richer than he was; he confiscated the temple and its money and burned at the stake every Templar knight he could round up. The knights were finished. Their fortified city-within-a-city lasted as a prison until it was destroyed in 1808. Two roads led to the temple enclosure, rue du Temple (Temple Rd.) and rue Vieille-du-Temple (Old Temple Rd.), and these are the only reminders of the Templars' presence in the Marais.

A serious uprising led by Etienne Marcel in 1357 caused the next monarch, Charles V, to leave his palace on the Ile de la Cité and move to the Marais, which was closer to possible escape routes. He installed his new royal residence between the Seine and rue St-Antoine near the Village St-Paul. His palace, the Hôtel St-Paul (later destroyed), was surrounded with a new wall that had the Bastille as its eastern rampart. The king's presence drew other wealthy, powerful people to settle in the Marais, but the turreted Hôtel de Sens and Hôtel de Clisson are the only buildings remaining from this period.

After the Hundred Years' War, Charles VII returned to Paris and chose to live in the Marais, occupying the Palais des Tournelles on the north side of place des Vosges. This was the royal residence of a series of French kings until Henri II was killed in a tournament there in 1559. His widow, Catherine de Médici, was so bereft she tore down the structure and replaced it with a horse market.

When Henri IV became king, he decided to turn the horse market into a grand square bordered by brick-and-stone pavilions where he intended to reside. The popular king was assassinated by Ravaillac in 1610, but his beautiful square, place Royal (now place des Vosges), became the centerpiece of

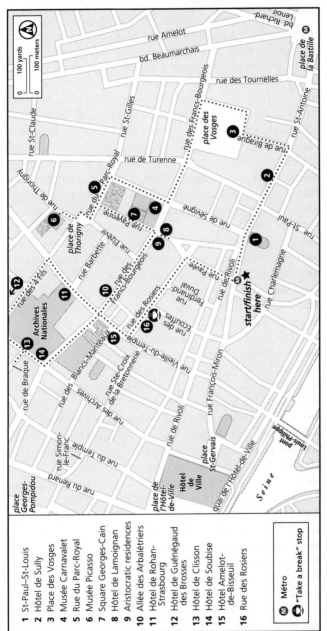

place de la Bastille

bd. Richard-Lenoir

rue Amelot

bd. Beaumarchais

rue des Tournelles

rue des Francs-Bourgeois

rue St-Gilles

rue St-Claude

rue de Thorigny

rue du Parc-Royal

rue de Turenne

rue de Bragque

place des Vosges

rue St-Antoine

rue de Sévigné

rue St-Paul

place de Thorigny

rue Payenne

rue Elzévir

rue Barbette

rue des Francs-Bourgeois

rue de Rivoli

rue Charlemagne

rue Ferdinand Duval

rue Pavée

Archives Nationales

rue des 4 Fils

rue des Rosiers

rue des Écouffes

rue de Braque

rue des Blancs-Manteaux

rue Ste-Croix de la Bretonnerie

rue des Archives

rue de Rivoli

rue Vieille-du-Temple

rue François-Miron

place Georges-Pompidou

rue du Renard

rue Simon-le-Franc

rue du Temple

place de l'Hôtel-de-Ville

Hôtel de Ville

place St-Gervais

pont Louis-Philippe

quai de l'Hôtel-de-Ville

Seine

start/finish here

100 yards / 100 meters

1 St-Paul–St-Louis
2 Hôtel de Sully
3 Place des Vosges
4 Musée Carnavalet
5 Rue du Parc-Royal
6 Musée Picasso
7 Square Georges-Cain
8 Hôtel de Lamoignan
9 Aristocratic residences
10 Allée des Arbalétriers
11 Hôtel de Rohan-Strasbourg
12 Hôtel de Guénégaud des Brosses
13 Hôtel de Clisson
14 Hôtel de Soubise
15 Hôtel Amelot-de-Bisseuil
16 Rue des Rosiers

Ⓜ Métro
🔊 "Take a break" stop

an affluent new neighborhood. The golden age of the Marais had begun, and it continued throughout the 17th century.

Greater and lesser nobility, financiers, high members of the clergy, and assorted other power brokers of the 17th century all sought a *grand hôtel particulier* (mansion) in the Marais. The top architects, painters, and sculptors of the day—Le Vau, Mansart, Le Brun, and Coysevox—worked on the design and ornamentation of these residences. Since symmetry was the hallmark of 17th-century design, the architects went to great lengths to ensure that the effect was both harmonious and pleasing. There is a cluster of these mansions around rue des Francs-Bourgeois, and you'll note that they follow a distinct design. Their massive entrance doors, often topped with carved masks or bas-reliefs, are like arches of triumph through which carriages passed to enter a vast, beautifully proportioned courtyard. The main building is at the end of the enclosed courtyard, and sometimes (if the occupants could afford it) is flanked by right and left wings. Somehow these mansions managed to flaunt the importance of their owners while remaining true to the principles of classic architecture.

By the mid–18th century, the aristocracy was shifting over to the faubourg St-Germain (see Walking Tour 4), and the building boom in the Marais died out. When the Bastille fell in 1789, most of the noble residents were frightened into abandoning their mansions or renting them out. Throughout the 19th century, artisans, small industries, and manufacturers moved into the spacious hôtels, subdividing the rooms, installing machinery in the courtyards, adding ugly new extensions, and generally wreaking havoc.

The neighborhood became so run-down that Baron Haussmann couldn't be bothered to run boulevards through it in the 19th century, which at least spared the Marais more extreme damage. Not until the 1962 "Malraux law" did the sad deterioration of the Marais begin to reverse itself. Named for André Malraux, minister of culture at the time of its enactment, the new law outlined a plan to restore and protect the mansions. The neighborhood finally came back to life.

This walk takes you through the heart of Paris's royal quarter. Because many of the hôtels are used as libraries, archives, or cultural centers, you can enter and admire their courtyards—at least during the week. If you're around for special events or exhibits, take the opportunity to admire the opulent interiors.

In addition to the striking architecture and trendy stores around place des Vosges, you'll go into the bustling Jewish district, where homey delis, patisseries, and takeout falafel shops serve a community that has been here for 7 centuries.

• • • • • • • • • • • • • • • •

Begin your tour at the church of:

1. **St-Paul–St-Louis,** built between 1627 (Louis XIII laid the first stone) and 1641 by the Jesuits. On May 9, 1641, Cardinal Richelieu said the first mass here, and the church became the favorite place of worship for the Marais's elegant inhabitants. Henry II's mausoleum was here for many years, along with the hearts of Louis XIII, Louis XIV, and other aristocrats. Though most of the art originally housed here was taken during the revolution, Delacroix's *Christ in the Garden of Olives* remains in the left transept. Note that the holy water stoups on each side of the entrance were donated by Victor Hugo.

    On leaving the church, turn right on rue St-Antoine. Now packed with shops and cafes, this street had been an ancient Roman road leading east. On the left side of the street at **no. 62** is the:

2. **Hôtel de Sully,** one of Paris's most impressive mansions. The home was built in 1624 by affluent banker Mesme-Gallet, but it was Henri IV's minister, the duc de Sully, who beautified it throughout with painted ceilings and painted and gilded pilasters. The facades and courtyard are richly ornamented in Renaissance style, with bas-reliefs representing the elements and the seasons. Sully was 74 when he bought this house, but he had a very young wife. "Here's so much for the household, so much for you, and so much for your lovers," he'd say when he gave her money, asking only that her lovers not loiter on his stairway.

    The building is now home to the Caisse Nationale des Monuments Historiques et des Sites (National Historical Monuments and Sites Commission), and temporary exhibitions are occasionally held here. (*An interesting footnote:* Voltaire was beaten by the servants of a nobleman under the portal here, sparking a series of events that led

to his imprisonment in the Bastille and exile to England.)
The building is open Monday to Saturday 8am to 7pm.

Turn left onto rue Birague, and this takes you on to:

3. **Place des Vosges,** one of the all-time great architectural ensembles. Thirty-six brick-and-stone pavilions rise
from graceful arcades surrounding the central square. The
buildings were constructed according to a strict plan—the
height of the facades is equal to their width, and the
height of the triangular roofs is half the height of the
facades—producing a remarkably symmetrical and harmonious space. The square was the model for Covent
Garden in London. Inaugurated on April 5, 6, and 7 in
1609, this was the first public square built by Henri IV
and was called place Royal. Henri intended it to be the
scene of both commercial business and social festivities.
Unfortunately, the "Vert Galant" never lived to see its
completion—he was assassinated 2 years before the square
opened—but the square continued to attract aristocratic
families throughout the 17th-century reign of Louis XIII.
During the revolution, the square became place de
l'Invisibilité, and its statue of Louis XIII was stolen (and
probably melted down); at this time it was also used as a
military site. Today, a replacement statue of Louis XIII
stands at the center of the square.

The square was renamed place des Vosges (the Vosges
département was the first in France to pay its taxes to
Napoléon) on September 23, 1800, and then it suffered
through a long period of decline with the rest of the
Marais. The 1962 "Malraux law" salvaged it, but you'll
notice that some of the pavilions are in better condition
than others. The restoration work is a continuing project.

Today, place des Vosges is once again the center of the
action. The vaulted arcades house antiques shops, bookstores, art galleries, and tea salons. You might even come
across a parade of musicians or a singer taking advantage
of the good acoustics under the arches.

You entered the square at **no. 1,** the Pavillon du Roi.
Despite its name, this was never a royal residence. Among
the decorative features, notice the sculpted head of Henri
IV in a medallion over the first floor.

To your left, **no. 1 bis** was the birthplace in 1626 of the marquise de Sévigné, famous in French literature for the series of letters she wrote her daughter. Take a few steps more to the left and you'll get to **no. 9,** which is the **Hôtel de Chaulnes,** with a spacious courtyard surrounding a fountain. It now houses one of the best restaurants in Paris: chef Bernard Pacaud's **L'Ambroisie** (call for reservations up to 1 month in advance; ✆ **01-42-78-51-45**). Many Parisians consider this restaurant the most romantic—and expensive—eatery in the city. President Clinton and his wife, Hillary, dined here in the late 1990s.

Proceed to your right (counterclockwise) to **no. 6,** the **Musée Victor-Hugo,** housed in the Hôtel de Rohan-Guéménée, where Hugo lived from 1832 to 1848. Inside are hundreds of books and drawings donated to the city in 1902 by Paul Meurice, Hugo's friend and the executor of his will. This museum owns more than 500 of Hugo's "spontaneous drawings," which are rotated regularly; it also possesses every edition of Hugo's works.

No. 8 is the former residence of authors Théophile Gautier (who wrote the libretto for the ballet *Giselle*) and Alphonse Daudet (who wrote the play *L'Arlessienne,* for which Georges Bizet provided the music). For more on Gautier, see Part II of Walking Tour 6, Stop 17.

As you continue around the square, note that **no. 14** was the mansion of the bishop of Langres; it once had splendid ceilings painted by Le Brun, now housed in the Musée Carnavalet (see the next stop). The building is now an Ashkenazic temple. Also note **no. 28,** the **Pavillon de la Reine,** one of the most fashionable hôtels in this area, with a lovely, ivy-covered courtyard.

No. 21 is another of Alphonse Daudet's homes, but this is more notable as the address of Armand-Jean du Plessis, duc de Richelieu, best known as Cardinal Richelieu (1585–1642), the power behind Louis XIII's throne. Richelieu was living here when he was appointed prime minister by Louis XIII in 1624. He later founded the Académie Française, built the Palais Royal, and began the Jardin des Plantes. Richelieu had such influence over the king that Louis XIII had his own mother, Marie de Médici, exiled when she opposed the cardinal.

Leave the square at the corner and you'll be on rue des Francs-Bourgeois, one of the best shopping streets in Paris for fashion, jewelry, and objets d'art. Make a right on rue de Sévigné. The sprawling corner building is the:

4. **Musée Carnavalet,** the museum of the history of Paris, housed in the Hôtel Carnavalet, a 16th-century mansion occupied by Mme de Sévigné during the last 19 years of her life. The building's overall style is due to the 17th-century owner, Claude Boislève, who hired celebrated architect François Mansart to enlarge and modernize the original. You can appreciate Mansart's Renaissance design in the courtyard even without visiting the museum. In addition to the lions over the main entrance, the bas-reliefs of the seasons and the zodiac signs in the courtyard were carved in the 16th century by Jean Goujon. The courtyard's left side portrays the elements in bas-reliefs, and its right side is adorned with four figures of sculpted divinities by Gérard Van Obstal. The statue in the center of a bewigged Louis XIV is by Coysevox. Inside, the exhibits of paintings, sculptures, decorative arts, and period costumes take you from Roman times through the Middle Ages through the Renaissance and up to the present. The highlights are Rooms 19 and 20, which were transported to the museum from the Hôtel La Rivière on place des Vosges. Note the extraordinary ceiling painted by Charles Le Brun depicting Psyche with eight Muses. The museum is open Tuesday to Sunday 10am to 5:40pm and there's an admission fee.

When you exit the museum, turn left on rue Sévigné, and at **no. 29** you'll pass the **Hôtel Le-Peletier-de-St-Fargeau,** which is linked to the Musée Carnavalet.

On the right side of rue de Sévigné, notice at **no. 48** the 1806 bas-relief representing Charity carved by Fortin and the masks and carvings at **no. 52,** the **Hôtel de Flesselles.**

Continue along rue de Sévigné until you reach:

5. **Rue du Parc-Royal.** Most of the mansions here were built between 1618 and 1620 by architect Jean Thiriot. Ahead, **no. 4** is the 17th-century **Hôtel de Canillac.** Continue left. **Nos. 6** and **8** were restored beyond recognition in the 19th century. **No. 10** is the **Hôtel de Vigny,**

symbolizing the area's twisting fortunes. When its wealthy inhabitants abandoned the residence at the end of the 18th century, the mansion, like many in the Marais, was turned over to industry. In this case, the building was occupied by a jeweler and suffered serious damage. It was scheduled for demolition in 1960, but workers discovered a startling 17th-century painted ceiling under coats of plaster. The mansion was saved and the movement to revitalize the Marais was born. Though you can't view the ceiling, an entrance to the left of the courtyard allows you to admire an intricate wrought-iron stair ramp. **No. 12** aged poorly over the centuries and was completely remodeled in 1988. Across the street you'll find a lovely manicured garden in the square Leopold-Achille, where there's also a playground and sandbox for kids. The shady benches are perfect for a little rest and contemplation.

Continue on rue du Parc-Royal to place de Thorigny and make a right on rue de Thorigny. Proceed to **no. 5,** which is the:

6. **Musée Picasso,** housed in the Hôtel Salé. On the artist's death in 1973, his heirs donated a collection of his work in lieu of inheritance taxes. The state acquired 203 paintings, 158 sculptures, 16 collages, and more than 3,000 drawings and etchings that are shown in rotation beneath the cherub-encrusted ceilings of this opulent mansion. The museum is open Wednesday to Monday 9:30am to 6pm (to 5:30pm in winter), and there's an admission fee.

An interesting note: The Hôtel Salé is the only mansion in the Marais not named after one of its owners. *Salé* means "salty" and refers to the source of Pierre Aubert de Fontenay's wealth. The mansion was built by M. de Fontenay out of his earnings as a *fermier général,* the choicest job in 17th-century France. *Fermiers généraux* controlled the distribution of salt throughout Paris and extracted a high price for that basic commodity. As a result, they were the richest—and most hated—men in town.

Retrace your steps to the corner of rue du Parc-Royal and rue Payenne. On your left, you'll see the:

7. **Square Georges-Cain,** both a delightful flowery park and the final resting place of important old stones. On the

left border is the orangerie of the Hôtel Le-Peletier-de-St-Fargeau, and ahead is the sculpted facade of the same mansion. On the right is a pediment from the former Palais des Tuileries. On the other side of the street at **no. 13** is the 17th-century **Hôtel du Lude,** also known as the **Hôtel de Châtillon.** Go into the rustic courtyard and on your right is a vestibule with a superb wrought-iron stairway and gate. Notice the mask over the entrance to the neighboring **Hôtel de Marle** at **no. 11.** Now occupied by the Swedish Cultural Institute, the mansion is notable for an unusual roof in the shape of an upside-down boat that you can see in the courtyard.

No. 5 has been turned into a somewhat strange shrine to Auguste Comte, the French philosopher who founded a school of thought known as positivism and coined the word *sociology.* His system for social reform is described in *The Course of Positive Philosophy* (1830–42), and *The System of Positive Polity* (1851–54) describes his belief in a society that makes a religion out of worshipping humanity. His Brazilian followers bought this 17th-century building and transformed it into La Chapelle de l'Humanité. The walls of the second-floor "chapel" are painted with portraits of the artists and thinkers who represented the ideals of positivism. You can go inside from Tuesday to Saturday between 3 and 6pm.

Follow rue Payenne across rue des Francs-Bourgeois until it becomes rue Pavée. At **no. 24** is the entrance to one of the oldest mansions of the Marais, the:

8. **Hôtel de Lamoignan,** built in 1585 for Diane de France, the illegitimate daughter of Henry II (made legitimate at age 7 by an adoption that granted her all noble rights), who lived here until her death. The first lady of the house is recalled in the motifs of the hunter-goddess Diana decorating the courtyard. The curved pediments are embellished with dogs' heads, bows and arrows, quivers, and other emblems of the hunt.

From 1658 to 1677, the hôtel was rented to Guillaume de Lamoignon, the first president of the Parliament of Paris. Over the door, the chubby cherubs holding a mirror and a serpent represent Truth and Prudence, words that may have been useful to a

Lamoignon descendant, Malesherbes, who defended Louis XVI before the revolutionary Tribunal.

The building, with an extension built in the 1960s, now houses the Bibliothèque Historique de la Ville de Paris.

Return to rue des Francs-Bourgeois and turn left to see a series of:

9. **Aristocratic residences.** The first building on your left at **nos. 29–31** is the **Hôtel d'Albret.** Built in 1563 for the high constable Anne de Montmorency, this mansion changed hands a number of times, with each owner contributing to its design. The rococo facade on the street dates from the 18th century, but the main building in the courtyard is original. The 16th-century left wing had been pierced with a passage that allowed carriages to enter the building directly, and the right wing was built in the 17th century. Eighteenth-century renovations tied the whole ensemble into a pleasing unity.

A number of celebrated figures were received here, and in the 17th century the mansion was the scene of a royal domestic drama. Mme de Montespan was the mistress of Louis XIV at the time of a soiree here when she met the marquise de Maintenon, the widow of a playwright. The mistress Montespan appointed the widow Maintenon governess of her children, only to be replaced as the object of the king's favor by the brainier marquise.

Next at **no. 33** is the **Hôtel Barbes,** built around 1634 but located behind an unfortunate 19th-century facade. **Nos. 35–37** is the **Hôtel de Coulanges,** where the marquise de Sévigné was raised by her uncle Philippe de Coulanges; it's now occupied by the cultural organization Maison de l'Europe.

Across the street at **no. 26** is the **Hôtel de Sandreville,** with a neoclassical facade dating from 1767. The brick-and-stone facade at **no. 30,** the 17th-century **Hôtel d'Alméras,** recalls the houses on place des Vosges. Notice the sculpted rams' heads around the door. If you buzz into the courtyard, you'll see a bust of Henri IV. The **Hôtel Poussepin** at **nos. 34–36** was built at the site of a 14th-century almshouse that gave the street its name—the 48 poor people sheltered here were known as "people who pay no tax" or *francs-bourgeois.* The benefactor of this worthy enterprise, a man named Le Mazurier, was soon complaining that his charges spent their days insulting and annoying passersby and their nights deafening their neighbors with noise. The place has become "an asylum of debauchery and prostitution," he wrote. The attractive courtyard now leads to the Swiss Cultural Center.

Next door at **no. 38** is the unusual:

10. **Allée des Arbalétriers,** a typical medieval street of large paving stones and overhanging upper stories. The lane once served as a secondary entrance to the Hôtel de Barbiette, the 14th-century mansion where Isabelle of Bavaria resided with her husband, Charles VI (France's most certifiably crazy king). On November 23, 1407, the king's brother, Louis d'Orléans, was returning to the hôtel through this alley when he was set upon by a gang. Men pulled him from his mule and hacked at him with swords and axes, leaving him to die in the gutter. The killers were hired by Jean the Fearless, duc de Bourgogne, and the murder launched 30 years of bitter conflict between the Burgundians and the Orléanists (Armagnacs).

Go right onto **rue Vieille-du-Temple.** On the corner a late-Gothic turret is all that remains of the Hôtel Hérouet, built around 1510. At **no. 87** is the entrance to the:

11. **Hôtel de Rohan-Strasbourg,** which, with the Hôtel de Soubise (below), represents the summit of what money could buy in the 18th-century Marais. These linked mansions were built around the same time and by the same architect, Delamair, for the powerful Rohan-Soubise clan. The mansions are spectacular in different ways. The Hôtel de Rohan-Strasbourg was built for the Cardinal de Rohan, bishop of Strasbourg, which perhaps explains its greater sobriety. The main courtyard, characterized by an austere classicism, opens onto the former stables on the right. This inner court contains one of the finest sculptures of 18th-century France, *The Watering of the Horses of the Sun,* which includes a nude Apollo and four horses against a background of exploding sunbursts. Inside, the main attraction is the amusing 18th-century Salon des Singes (Monkey Room); however, the interior is open to the public only during exhibitions. Along with the Hôtel de Soubise (below), this mansion is now home to the

National Archives. The courtyard is open Monday to Saturday 9am to 5pm.

At the corner, turn left onto rue des 4 Fils and continue to the corner of rue des Archives and turn right. Near the corner, at **no. 60,** is the entrance to the Musée de la Chasse et Nature (Museum of Hunting and Nature), lodged in the:

12. **Hôtel de Guénégaud des Brosses.** This imposing manor was constructed by the great architect François Mansart, uncle of Jules-Hardouin Mansart, who designed the dome of the Hôtel des Invalides and other works for Louis XIV. The museum, open Wednesday to Monday 10am to 12:30pm and 1:30 to 5:30pm (there's an admission fee), houses an interesting collection of 17th-century hunting weapons such as rifles inlaid with pearls and engraved with ivory.

Retrace your steps and notice the 18th-century **fountain** with the sculpted nymph on the southwest corner of rue des Archives and rue des Haudriettes. Continue down rue des Archives. On your left at **no. 58** are the cone-shaped towers of the former:

13. **Hôtel de Clisson.** The towers are all that remain of the 14th-century Clisson mansion and are one of the few remnants in Paris of medieval defensive architecture. In 1553, the mansion was acquired by the ducs de Guise, who were rabidly anti-Protestant and opposed any and all attempts on the part of Catherine de Médici toward reconciliation with the Huguenots. It was probably in this house that the St. Bartholomew's Day Massacre was organized. The colorful medallions over the door were added in the 19th century.

Make a right on **rue de Braque,** and a few steps into this pretty street you'll notice the finely carved balcony supports at **nos. 4–6,** which is the **Hôtel Lelièvre.**

Return to rue des Archives, make a right, and then make a left at rue des Francs-Bourgeois to find at **no. 60** the entrance to the:

14. **Hôtel de Soubise,** which may be the highlight of your walk. This extraordinary palace was built in 1705 by François de Rohan, prince de Soubise, on the site of the

earlier Hôtel de Clisson (see above). The architect Delamair created an enormous courtyard enclosed by a 56-column peristyle and a promenade. The facade is adorned with reclining figures of Prudence and Wisdom and groups of children representing artistic spirits. Decorated in rococo style later in the same century, the interior includes works by Boucher, Natoire, and Van Loo.

Since 1808, the palace has contained the National Archives of France, which have since spread to adjoining buildings on rue des Francs-Bourgeois as well as the Hôtel de Rohan-Strasbourg (see above). The first floor is devoted to the Musée de l'Histoire de France (Historical Museum of France), displaying documents like the 1598 Edict of Nantes, the Declaration of Human Rights, and Napoléon's will, as well as a stone model of the Bastille. Even if you choose not to visit the museum, take a walk across the courtyard to the entry hall, in which Zeus probably would have felt comfortable. You can visit the courtyard Monday to Friday 9am to 7pm and Saturday and Sunday 2 to 5pm. The museum is open Wednesday to Monday 2 to 5pm, and there's an admission fee.

When you leave the Hôtel de Soubise, make a left and continue along rue des Francs-Bourgeois. The 17th-century buildings on the left from **nos. 58–54** are part of the archives complex.

Make a right at rue Vieille-du-Temple and at **no. 47** you'll find the:

15. **Hôtel Amelot-de-Bisseuil,** also known as the **Hôtel des Ambassadeurs de Hollande,** even though no Dutch ambassadors have ever lived there. It was here that Beaumarchais wrote *The Marriage of Figaro.* The popular author had his fingers in a lot of pies; while writing controversial plays that made fun of the aristocracy, Beaumarchais was also involved in financing and organizing the shipment of arms to American revolutionaries. The ground floor of this mansion is now occupied by offices. During working hours you can ring into the outer courtyard and gaze at a profusion of sculptures and bas-reliefs, most notably that of Romulus and Remus over the inside entry door.

After the Hôtel Amelot-de-Bisseuil, turn left on:

16. **Rue des Rosiers,** the heart of the old Jewish quarter. The Jewish community in this neighborhood dates from the 13th century—references to the "street of rosebushes" *(rosiers)* were found as early as 1230. Though the Jewish presence in Paris is as ancient as the city itself, this neighborhood was settled after Philippe-Auguste expelled the Jews from Paris in 1183 and the community took up residence here, outside the city walls. Despite periodic pogroms and expulsions, the Jewish community retained strong links to the neighborhood. A census in 1808 showed that 82% of Parisian Jews lived in the Marais. Around that time, the community was swelling with an Ashkenazi population made up of refugees, especially from Poland, Russia, and Austria. The community was decimated during the Holocaust; much of their property and many businesses were confiscated. Since the war, the neighborhood has seen an influx of Sephardic Jews from France's former colonies in North Africa—as well as an influx of tourists from everywhere. The shops still have signs in Hebrew, and there's no better place in Paris to experience eastern European cuisine.

Notice the old houses at **nos. 32, 23, 20,** and **18.** At **no. 4** is the **Hammam,** or Jewish Public Baths.

Take a Break At no. 7 rue des Rosiers is **Chez Jo Goldenberg,** founded by Albert Goldenberg. You can't miss it; its window displays (consisting mainly of hanging sausages) are unusual for Paris. Here you can lunch on chopped liver, pastrami, or gefilte fish. The place can get so full that you sometimes need to make a reservation. Still, there's no harm in trying to get in without one.

If unsuccessful, you might instead stop for falafel at **Le Roi du Falaffel–Rosiers Alimentation** at **no. 4,** or any similar place along the way. Near Chez Jo Goldenberg at **no. 27** is **Finkelsztajn.** Established in 1851, this is one of the city's finest Jewish pastry shops. You'll probably have to fight crowds to get in, but the desserts are worth the effort.

You'll probably want to stroll down the side streets, **rue des Ecouffes** and **rue Ferdinand-Duval,** before turning right on **rue Pavée** at the end of rue des Rosiers. On the left at **no. 10** is the **synagogue** built in 1913 by Art Nouveau master Hector Guimard.

A Parisian *Pique-nique*

One of the best ways to enjoy Parisian cuisine is to picnic. Go to a *fromagerie* for cheese; to a *boulangerie* for a baguette; to a charcuterie for pâté, sausage, or salad; and to a patisserie for luscious pastries. Add a bottle of Côtes du Rhone—it goes well with picnics—and you'll have the makings of a delightful, typically French meal you can take to the nearest park or along the banks of the Seine. Pretend you're in Manet's *Déjeuner sur l'herbe* and enjoy! (Don't forget the corkscrew!)

The best spot for a picnic is a cozy nook along the **Seine.** Another great place for picnics (also boating, walks, and jogging) is the **Bois de Boulogne** (Métro: Porte Maillot), covering some 2,000 acres at the western edge of Paris. At night it becomes a twilight zone of sex and drugs, but it's lovely during the day. Even though they're in a state of restoration, the splendid gardens of **Versailles** offer another fine picnic spot. You can also enjoy your meal on the grass on a day trip to the cathedral city of **Chartres.** Go to bucolic **Parc André Gagon,** a 5-minute walk northwest of the fabled cathedral.

At the end of the street you'll be at the St-Paul Métro station, which is the start of Part II.

PART II   THE SOUTHERN MARAIS & ILE ST-LOUIS

Start: St-Paul Métro station.

Finish: Intersection of rue St-Louis-en-l'Ile and rue des Deux-Ponts.

Time: About 3 hours.

Best Time: Thursday to Saturday, if you can manage it.

Worst Time: Tuesday and Wednesday, when the antiques shops and stalls of the Village St-Paul are closed (though the village itself is open), or Sunday and Monday, when the courtyard of the Hôtel de Sens is closed.

The south Marais is both less touristed and more residential than the royal Marais. Like the neighborhood north of rue St-Antoine, it was protected by the 13th-century wall built by Philippe-Auguste and then flourished in the 14th century when Charles V built his palace complex near the Village St-Paul. Though you'll see several stunning 17th-century mansions here, this neighborhood has a quieter, more intimate flavor than its northern neighbor.

When you cross the bridge onto the Ile St-Louis, the mood changes dramatically. The island was developed in the 17th century as an annex to the fashionable Marais, but unlike the Marais it never went out of style. While the Marais industrialized in the 19th century, the Ile St-Louis hosted poets and writers lured by the elegant architecture. Few poets and writers can afford to live on the island now, however. Its population is predominantly made up of visitors, extremely well-heeled residents, and proprietors of ceramics shops. Even if its quaintness is becoming self-conscious, this island remains a well-preserved ensemble of 17th-century architecture marvelously located in the middle of the Seine.

• • • • • • • • • • • • • • • • •

Begin at the St-Paul Métro station and take:

1. **Rue François-Miron** to the left of the Pier Import store. Like rue St-Antoine, which it joins, rue François-Miron was an ancient Roman road that led east to Rome. Now it's the south Marais's main commercial street. On your left at **no. 82** is the **Hôtel Hénault de Cantobre,** now the Maison Européen de la Photographie.

    No. 68 is the **Hôtel de Beauvais,** built in 1654 for Catherine Bellier. Known as "One-eyed Kate," this lady-in-waiting to Anne of Austria was the first mistress of the 16-year-old Louis XIV. The king was so enamored with her that both she and her husband were showered with gifts. He became counselor to the king and then a baron, while Catherine was presented with a large fortune that she used to buy a piece of property and build this mansion.

    The mansion eventually became the residence of the Bavarian ambassador. In 1763, Wolfgang Amadeus

Mozart, his father, and his sister stayed here on the second floor for 5 months while the 7-year-old prodigy enchanted all Paris with his genius. Sadly, it has become rather dilapidated and is undergoing extensive reconstruction.

The 16th-century house at **nos. 44–46** used to be the Ourscamp abbey but now belongs to the **Association du Paris Historique,** which has restored the structure. The association runs an information center here and allows free visits to the vaulted Gothic cellars that date from 1250. It's open Monday to Saturday 2 to 6pm.

Not everyone in the Marais lived in mansions with carriage gates and sculpted facades. Notice the disheveled half-timber houses at **nos. 11** and **13.** They date from around the end of the 15th century, before a municipal ordinance forbade timber construction as a fire hazard and ordered that all half-timber houses be covered with a layer of plaster. The outer coat of plaster has been removed as part of a restoration project, providing a rare glimpse of a humble medieval residence.

The ensemble of buildings that ranges from **nos. 14** to **2** was constructed in 1732 for the use of the church of St-Gervais–St-Protais. The most stylish is **no. 14,** by architect Jacques-Ange Gabriel, who designed place de la Concorde. Notice the old street name carved into the facade, RUE DE POUR TOUR, and the elm in wrought iron on the first-floor balcony of each building.

The symbol of the elm is very closely linked with the church of:

2. **St-Gervais–St-Protais.** As you round the corner, you'll see a small elm in the center of the St-Gervais square in front of the church. Until the revolution, debts and claims were settled under an elm here. Judges held court in the square and the parish priest published their edicts. A promise made "under the elm" was supposed to be inviolable.

The origins of St-Gervais–St-Protais lie in the 6th century, when a basilica was erected here to saints Gervase and Protase, two Roman officers martyred by Nero. The church was reconstructed in the 13th and 17th centuries, but little remains of the older structure. The classical facade with Doric, Ionic, and Corinthian orders was the first of its kind in Paris and was built by Métezeau in

The Southern Marais & Ile St-Louis

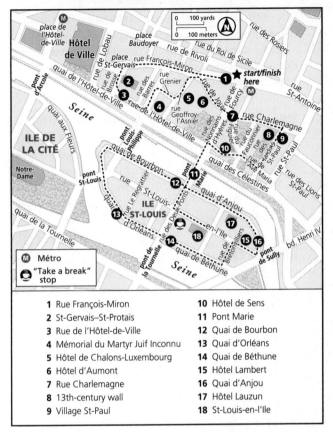

1 Rue François-Miron	**10** Hôtel de Sens
2 St-Gervais–St-Protais	**11** Pont Marie
3 Rue de l'Hôtel-de-Ville	**12** Quai de Bourbon
4 Mémorial du Martyr Juif Inconnu	**13** Quai d'Orléans
5 Hôtel de Chalons-Luxembourg	**14** Quai de Béthune
6 Hôtel d'Aumont	**15** Hôtel Lambert
7 Rue Charlemagne	**16** Quai d'Anjou
8 13th-century wall	**17** Hôtel Lauzun
9 Village St-Paul	**18** St-Louis-en-l'Ile

1621. From 1656 to 1826, members of the great Couperin family of organists played the organ here.

The interior is bright, with Flamboyant Gothic vaulting, stained-glass windows, and carved stalls—all dating from the 16th and 17th centuries. The nave of the church was hit by German artillery on March 29, 1918, causing 100 deaths, but it was well reconstructed.

Coming out of the church, follow rue de Brosse and make a left onto:

3. **Rue de l'Hôtel-de-Ville.** This winding street had been called rue de la Mortellerie after the medieval masons (*morteliers*) who used to live here. After a cholera epidemic in 1832 killed 19,000 Parisians in 90 days, the neighborhood residents demanded a name that didn't contain

the word *mort* (death). At **no. 89** you can see the former name still inscribed on the building.

Make a left and mount the tranquil 13th-century **rue des Barres.** Make a right at **no. 12,** which was part of the Maubuisson abbey, onto rue Grenier-sur-l'Eau. Continue to rue Geoffroy-l'Asnier. To your right at **no. 17** is the:

4. **Mémorial du Martyr Juif Inconnu (Memorial to the Unknown Jew),** in which an eternal flame burns in commemoration of Jewish victims of the Holocaust. The museum also contains archives devoted to Jewish history. It's open Sunday to Friday 10am to 1pm and 2 to 6pm. There's an admission fee.

Make a left at **no. 26** and you'll see the dramatic entrance to the:

5. **Hôtel de Chalons-Luxembourg.** A fierce lion appears to be eating a dish over the towering doorway. The court-yard facade has the initials P and B in bas-relief—a reminder that the mansion was built for Guillaume Perrochel and his wife Françoise Buisson. This house is an excellent example of 17th-century brick-and-stone style.

Continue up rue Geoffroy-l'Asnier and make a sharp right onto rue François-Miron, continuing to **rue de Jouy,** which was named after an abbey that had a house here. On your right at **no. 7** is the:

6. **Hôtel d'Aumont,** assembled by two of the finest names in 17th-century design. Louis Le Vau, who worked on the Louvre and Versailles, planned the first building. François Mansart, who touched up the Hôtel Carnavalet (now the Musée Carnavalet; see Part I, Stop 4), installed the facade on the garden, which you can see through a gate. The classic lines of the courtyard are worth a look.

When you come out of the courtyard, notice the amusing carving of the knife-grinder on the facade at the left corner of rue de Jouy and rue de Fourcy. A modern building replaced the 17th-century knife-grinding shop, but luckily the carving was remounted on the facade.

Cross rue de Fourcy. The street becomes:

7. **Rue Charlemagne.** At **no. 18** lived an 18th-century judge who had a reputation for allowing gifts of fresh eggs and capons to influence his decisions. Next is a high

school, the **Lycée Charlemagne,** on the site of a 13th-century convent known for its extraordinary severity. The sisters at the Ave Maria convent were required to remain barefoot, sleep on the ground, pray between midnight and 3am, and wear a veil even in the presence of their families.

Notice the charming 19th-century **fountain** at **no. 8** topped by the coat-of-arms of Paris. Continue on about 15m (50 ft.) and take a stroll down little **rue Eginhard,** between **nos. 4** and **6.** Return to the fountain on rue Charlemagne and make a left onto rue des Jardins St-Paul. On your right is the largest remaining fragment of Philippe-Auguste's:

8. **13th-century wall,** which once enclosed the neighborhood. On the corner of rue Charlemagne is a piece of the Tour Montgomery, named after the man who accidentally mortally wounded Henri II in a tournament in 1559. He was probably held here.

   Continue down the street and on your left you'll see entrances to the:

9. **Village St-Paul,** a secluded 17th-century village turned outdoor arts fair. Take some time to explore the interlocking courtyards lined with shops selling antiques, paintings, and bric-a-brac. The haphazard arrangement of courtyards dates from the 14th century, when they were the walled gardens of Charles V. When the palace was abandoned, townspeople built houses along the walls, and the gardens became their village squares. Special flea markets are usually held each spring and fall, drawing vendors from the Paris region. The stores are open Thursday to Monday 11am to 7pm.

   Leave the village on the same street, rue des Jardins St-Paul, and continue left to rue de l'Ave Maria, where you turn right. Turn right after the square de l'Ave Maria, onto rue du Figuier, and at **no. 1** you'll see the towers and turrets of the:

10. **Hôtel de Sens.** With its Gothic portal, framed by two turrets, this is one of the few surviving examples of medieval Parisian domestic architecture. Half fortress, half mansion, it was built from 1474 to 1519 as a residence for the powerful archbishops of Sens. The

Bourbons and the Guises then occupied the fortified mansion, using it as a stronghold for the Catholic League—the anti-Protestant group. In the late 16th century Henri IV sent his extravagant first wife, Queen Margot, here after they separated. The archbishops of Paris then resided here until the revolution and later rented it to art students and jam makers, who destroyed the interior. In 1916, the city took it over, and in 1936, after much controversy, a restoration project was begun. It took 26 years to complete. Presently the Hôtel de Sens houses the Bibliothèque Forney, which specializes in the fine arts, including decorative arts, crafts, and architecture. You can enter the impressive courtyard Tuesday to Friday 1:30 to 8:30pm and Saturday 10am to 8:30pm to admire the finely executed decoration.

Leaving the courtyard, turn right and follow rue de l'Hôtel-de-Ville around to the garden in back of the hôtel. To your left is:

11. **Pont Marie,** named after the real estate developer who created the Ile St-Louis (see below). Originally the bridge had some houses built along its sides, but in 1658 two of the arches collapsed and 22 houses disappeared into the river with them. Since 1788, the bridge has changed little.

As you cross the bridge you'll have an excellent view of the mansions along the quays of the **Ile St-Louis.** Nearly all the houses and mansions here were constructed between 1618 and 1660, lending the island a remarkable architectural unity. In 1360, the original island was cut in two by a canal (now rue Poulletier) that reinforced Philippe-Auguste's 13th-century wall. The eastern island was called Ile aux Vaches (Island of Cows) and was used for grazing, fishing, and washing clothes; the western island was called Ile Notre-Dame. Both islands were owned by the chapter of Notre-Dame. In 1614, engineer Christophe Marie signed with Louis XIII an agreement allowing him to join the two islands and connect the property with the right and left banks of the Seine. Since the Marais was becoming Paris's most sought-after real estate, Marie and his two partners envisioned a profitable development scheme that would attract the overflow.

Despite the opposition of the Notre-Dame chapter and squabbling among the partners, work proceeded relatively quickly, but the Marie team was later fired and replaced by the architect Louis Le Vau and his brother François. Because the island was developed according to a plan, the streets are straight and intersect at right angles—a rarity in Paris. The inner part of the island was quickly occupied by merchants and artisans, and rich magistrates and financiers snatched up the riverfront property, with spectacular views over the Seine. The desire for a river view dictated the style of the architecture. Unlike homes in the Marais, where the main building is hidden behind a gateway and a courtyard, the mansions of the Ile St-Louis have more windows and the main building is on the quay. The houses in the interior streets are modest by comparison but retain a great deal of old-world refinement.

From pont Marie, turn right along:

12. **Quai de Bourbon.** Christophe Marie installed *bateaux-lavoirs* (public laundries) along quai de Bourbon. Until the 1800s, the quay was lined with barges where women washed clothes in tubs of hot water and rinsed them in the Seine, which was probably not much cleaner than it is now.

   No. 1 was a cabaret for sailors until it was closed in 1716 for storing subversive pamphlets; its former business is evident in the grape-and-vine motif on the wrought-iron gate. Passing the sculpted masks on **no. 11,** which belonged to valet/painter Philippe de Champaigne, you'll come to the **Hôtel le Charron** at **nos. 13–15** and the **Hôtel de Jassaud** at **no. 19.** Both have the kind of facades that trumpeted the importance of their 17th-century occupants. Sculptor Camille Claudel lived and worked in the Hôtel de Jassaud from 1899 to 1913.

   At the corner of quai de Bourbon and rue Le Regrattier, you'll see a **headless statue.** Although rue Le Regrattier was originally named rue de la Femme Sans Tête (Street of the Headless Woman), the statue isn't of a woman at all but of St. Nicolas, the patron saint of boatmen. The "headless woman" is supposed to refer to an old sign showing a headless woman with a glass and the seemingly inappropriate slogan TOUT EST BON ("All is good"). No, I don't know what it means, either.

Continue along quai de Bourbon with its array of elegant mansions. **No. 25** was the home of French Socialist Léon Blum when he headed the leftist Popular Front government in 1936; **no. 27** was built for a nephew of Cardinal Mazarin—Louis XIV's influential minister. Near pont Louis-Philippe, **nos. 45, 47,** and **49** were built by and for the famous Le Vau brothers. **No. 45** is called the Maison du Centaure because of the two bas-reliefs in a medallion showing Hercules felling the Centaur.

The tip of the island is spectacularly scenic, with a view of St-Gervais–St-Protais on the Right Bank and (as you round the tip toward pont St-Louis) a view of the Ile de la Cité and Notre-Dame. Past the pedestrian pont St-Louis, quai de Bourbon becomes:

13. **Quai d'Orléans,** the name of another royal family. Along the quay you'll have a splendid view of the Left Bank and the Panthéon.

Nos. 18–20 is the **Hôtel Rolland,** where Walter Lippmann (1889–1974) and his wife lived for a short time in 1938. A journalist/editor who worked for the *New Republic,* the *Washington Post,* and the New York *Herald Tribune,* Lippmann was a 1958 Pulitzer Prize recipient. Author James Jones lived at **no. 10** from 1958 to 1975, eventually buying three floors in the house with the income from the film script for *The Longest Day.* When he wasn't entertaining a stream of writers and artists, Jones wrote *The Thin Red Line, A Touch of Danger,* and *Viet Journal* from his office behind the first-floor windows overlooking the Seine.

At **no. 6** is the **Musée Adam-Mickiewicz,** which you might find interesting if it's open (which it is on Thurs only, 2–6pm). Dedicated to the exiled poet known as the "Byron of Poland," the second-floor museum houses mementos as well as a library. On the ground floor is an entire room dedicated to Chopin—it even holds his old armchair.

Following the Polish uprising against Russia in 1831, the Ile St-Louis became a refuge for Polish immigrants. Exiled Prince Adam Czartoryski bought the Hôtel Lambert (see below) and turned it into a salon for Polish intellectuals and artists; Fréderic Chopin provided the music. His wife, Princess Czartoryska, founded a charitable organization for the émigrés as well as an institute to teach their daughters the Polish language and culture. The Polish library of this museum was created by the prince, and it remains one of the largest specialized libraries in Paris.

Continue straight onto:

14. **Quai de Béthune,** which had been called quai des Balcons after the number of overhanging balconies with which Louis Le Vau adorned his buildings. **Nos. 32, 30,** and **28** were built by Le Vau's father; notice at **no. 28** the bas-reliefs representing Sculpture, Painting, and Music. **No. 24** is the **Hôtel Hesselin.** Only the portal remains of the original Le Vau building, for the rest was destroyed and rebuilt in 1935 for Helena Rubinstein. Former President Georges Pompidou died here in April 1974. **No. 22** was the first residence of Baudelaire in 1842, and **nos. 16–18** belonged to the duc de Richelieu (great-nephew of the Cardinal), a handsome rake who became ambassador to Vienna.

Go left on rue Bretonvilliers, which was built as an access route to the Hôtel de Bretonvilliers, a magnificent mansion that covered most of the eastern tip of the island. The remaining vestiges of the hôtel were erased with the construction of pont Sully in 1876, except for the archway you'll pass through to go to rue St-Louis-en-l'Ile. Turn right to **no. 2,** which is the:

15. **Hôtel Lambert.** This 17th-century residence was Louis Le Vau's masterpiece, built in 1645 for Nicolas Lambert de Thorigny, president of the Chambre des Comptes. The portal on rue St-Louis-en-l'Ile gives some idea of the splendors within, but the mansion's most startling element is the oval gallery extending into the garden. Designed to feature either a library or an art collection, the gallery is best viewed from the beginning of quai d'Anjou.

At one time, Voltaire was a resident of the Hôtel Lambert with his mistress, Emilie de Breteuil, marquise de Châtelet. They had such raucous fights that they were talked about all over Europe. For a century, this was the home of Poland's royal family, the Czartoryskis (see above), before becoming the residence of the actress Michèle Morgan. It now belongs to the Rothschild family and isn't open to the public.

Continue right and turn left onto:

16. **Quai d'Anjou.** Notice **no. 3,** which was built at the same time as the Hôtel Lambert by Louis Le Vau and is linked to it by a large balcony. **Nos. 9, 11, 13,** and **15** also belonged to the Lambert family. **No. 9** is where sculptor/painter/caricaturist Honoré Daumier once lived. Most famous for his spontaneous caricatures of political figures, Daumier was even imprisoned for 6 months because of his 1832 cartoon showing Louis-Philippe swallowing bags of gold that had been extracted from his people.

Continue ahead to **no. 17,** which is the:

17. **Hôtel Lauzun,** another Louis Le Vau masterpiece. The hôtel's exterior doesn't look like much, but the interior is a splendid amalgamation of the plans of a group of architects, including Le Vau, Le Brun, Lepautre, and Bourdon. The painted ceilings and intricately carved wood paneling (*boiserie*) have been preserved, along with some statues, tapestries, and paintings.

Notwithstanding the splendor of the architecture and the decoration, the mansion seems to have brought bad luck on many of its inhabitants. It was built from 1656 to 1657 for Charles Gruyn des Bordes, whose father had made a fortune as the owner of the Ile de la Cité's popular Pomme de Pin cabaret, where Racine and Molière were frequent guests. The younger Gruyn (des Bordes was an aristocratic title he bought) married Geneviève de Mouy and lovingly engraved her initials on much of the interior decor. Their happiness was short-lived, however, for Gruyn was convicted of embezzlement in 1662 and sent to prison.

The next owner was the duc de Lauzun, who resided here for only 3 years. Lauzun had attracted the attention of Louis XIV's first cousin, the duchesse de Montpensier, who became enraptured and wished to marry him. Fearing that a union with the illustrious duchesse would make Lauzun more powerful than he deserved, Louis XIV refused to consent to the marriage and then, for good measure, threw Lauzun into prison, where he moldered for 10 years. The duchesse was inconsolable and finally managed to pester the king into releasing him. The two lovers married in secret, and Lauzun bought this mansion in 1682 as a residence for himself and his hard-won bride. Alas, domestic bliss eluded the couple. They fought often and finally separated in 1684.

Lauzun sold the house in 1685 to Louis-Armand du Plessis de Vignerod, the grand-nephew of Cardinal Richelieu, and his wife, who was the grand-niece of Cardinal Mazarin. This blue-blooded couple had such a good time throwing brilliant parties for all the notables of the day that they went bankrupt, separated, and had to sell their house.

Bibliophile/collector Baron Pichon bought the mansion in 1842 and rented it out to a hashish club. Tenants Baudelaire and Théophile Gautier regularly held hashish soirees in which Baudelaire did the research for *Les Paradis artificiels* (loosely translated, "drug-induced states of fantasy"). Gautier recounted his experiences in his *Le Club des hachichins.* The hôtel is now owned by the City of Paris, which is doing restoration work until sometime in 2006. The spectacular interior is occasionally open for temporary exhibits. Call the tourist office at © **08-92-68-31-12** for further information.

Continue along the quay and go left at rue des Deux-Ponts and make a left on **rue St-Louis-en-l'Ile.** One of the first streets you reach, rue St-Louis-en-l'Ile, contains few mansions but many shops and restaurants and several charming little hotels. Some of the stores are a bit precious, but this might be just the place to find that unusual piece of jewelry or luminescent vase. At **no. 19 bis** is the island's star attraction, the church of:

18. **St-Louis-en-l'Ile.** Despite its somewhat dour exterior, this church's ornate interior is one of the finest examples of Jesuit Baroque style. Built between 1664 and 1726 according to Louis Le Vau's original designs, the church has been—and still is—the site of many Parisian weddings. It's no wonder; with all this white stone and gilt, visitors feel a bit like they have stepped into a giant wedding cake. Amid the marble and woodwork you'll find a glazed terra-cotta statue of St. Louis, as well as a 1926 plaque reading IN GRATEFUL MEMORY OF ST. LOUIS IN

WHOSE HONOR THE CITY OF ST. LOUIS, MISSOURI, USA, IS NAMED. Note the iron clock at the church entrance, as well as the iron spire, dating from 1765.

Take a Break At no. 31 rue St-Louis-en-l'Ile (on the corner of rue des Deux-Ponts) is **Berthillon,** said by some to be the best ice-cream and sorbet parlor in all Europe. The ice-cream flavors range from standard chocolate and vanilla to Grand Marnier and mocha; sorbets range from lime to rhubarb. (Note that Berthillon's opening hours are erratic and the shop is sometimes closed for a week or longer in mid-summer.)

If it is closed, walk up rue St-Louis-en-l'Ile to **no. 90** and sample the cakes and quiches at the tea salon **Au Lys d'Argent.** For lunch or dinner, La Castafiore, at **no. 51,** is a delightful little restaurant serving excellent homemade pastas.

To find the St-Paul Métro station, cross pont Marie and continue straight on rue des Nonnains d'Hyères, which becomes rue de Fourcy. The Métro is to your right on rue St-Antoine.

The Faubourg St-Germain

Start: Place de la Concorde (Métro: Concorde).

Finish: Hôtel de Seignelay.

Time: 4 to 6 hours.

Best Time: Tuesday to Sunday for the Musée d'Orsay and Musée Rodin, and Saturday for the Palais Bourbon.

Worst Time: Monday, when the museums are closed.

The faubourg St-Germain is on the Left Bank, but its ambience is as decorous as that of any Right Bank enclave. Gourmet food shops, galleries, florists, and boutiques serve the city's most upscale clientele. At the core of the neighborhood are 18th-century *hôtels particuliers* (mansions), each more splendid than the next. Now that they've been converted to government buildings and embassies, the area has taken on an "official" character that's more than a little uptight. It has been called Washington-sur-Seine, a neighborhood that exudes power and confidence. It creates a perfect setting for the prime minister's palace, the Hôtel de Matignon, and the glorious Musée d'Orsay and Musée Rodin.

The faubourg St-Germain owes its name to its origin as a *faubourg* (suburb) of the old town of St-Germain, which had grown around the abbey of St-Germain-des-Prés. Until the reign of Henri IV, the faubourg was little more than a vast field (*prés*), but in the early 17th century various convents and orders moved here, and the quarter slowly became populated.

When Catherine de Médici decided to build the Palais des Tuileries in 1564, it became clear that the Right Bank needed a link to the quarries in south Paris. A ferry service (*bac*) was instituted and a road built to carry stones to the ferry (this became known as rue du Bac). As far as the aristocracy was concerned, the new road meant that the faubourg was no longer in the boondocks, but conveniently connected to the center of royal power. Country lanes like rue de Grenelle and rue de Varenne that connected with rue du Bac moved rapidly upscale—and have stayed stylish ever since.

By the 18th century, the faubourg St-Germain replaced the Marais as Paris's most coveted real estate. Rue du Bac led to rue de Vaugirard, which led to Versailles—the source of titles, privileges, kingly favors, and all the other goodies Louis XIV could dispense. Luxurious hôtels bloomed around the neighborhood and were occupied by the pride of the *ancien régime*—like the duchesse de Bourbon, duchesse de Maine, duc de Castries, comte de Matignon, and princesse de Bourbon-Condé.

Everything changed with the revolution. The illustrious names fled for their lives; the mansions were auctioned off or even dangled as prizes in the National Lottery. When Napoléon came to power, his family and associates, such as Talleyrand, once again filled the comfortable and convenient residences. With the restoration of the monarchy in 1815, the aristocracy trickled back to their old district, but soon the faubourg St-Germain was competing for upscale occupants with the faubourg St-Honoré and, later, the Champs-Elysées.

The neighborhood remains one of the most expensive areas in Paris, not a place to expect bargains in food or anything else. Though this tour does not explore cobblestone alleys or meander through outdoor markets, the sheer number of extremely expensive hôtels speaks volumes about the concentration of power and wealth in pre-revolutionary France.

• • • • • • • • • • • • • • • •

The Faubourg St-Germain

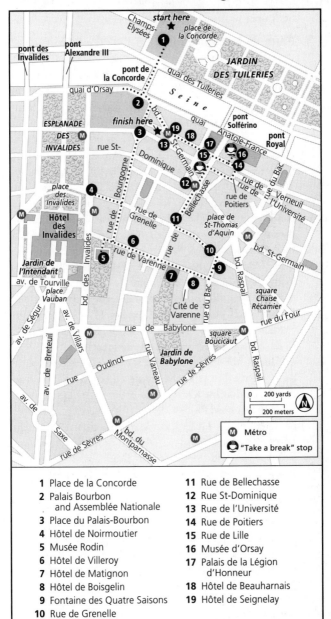

1 Place de la Concorde
2 Palais Bourbon
   and Assemblée Nationale
3 Place du Palais-Bourbon
4 Hôtel de Noirmoutier
5 Musée Rodin
6 Hôtel de Villeroy
7 Hôtel de Matignon
8 Hôtel de Boisgelin
9 Fontaine des Quatre Saisons
10 Rue de Grenelle

11 Rue de Bellechasse
12 Rue St-Dominique
13 Rue de l'Université
14 Rue de Poitiers
15 Rue de Lille
16 Musée d'Orsay
17 Palais de la Légion
   d'Honneur
18 Hôtel de Beauharnais
19 Hôtel de Seignelay

Start your walk at:

1. **Place de la Concorde.** Located at the southeast end of the Champs-Elysées, this may not be a restful place to sit and relax, but the harmony of the design and the sweeping vista up the avenue make it one of the grandest squares in Paris—if not the world. The 8.4-hectare (21-acre) octagonal space was designed by Jacques-Ange Gabriel in 1763 as a setting for a statue of Louis XV. Following the nature-loving spirit of the age, Gabriel refused to block off the tree-lined Seine, the Champs-Elysées, or the Jardin des Tuileries with buildings; instead, he built only on the square's northern side. Two majestic colonnaded palaces flank rue Royale. The right pavilion was the **royal furniture warehouse** where Marie Antoinette secretly used to stay when she visited Paris; it's now the Ministry of the Navy. Opposite is the superdeluxe **Hôtel de Crillon,** originally the residence of the comte de Crillon. It was here that the Treaty of Friendship and Trade recognizing the United States was signed in February 1778 by Benjamin Franklin and Louis XVI. The U.S. Embassy now sits next to the Hôtel de Crillon, just off the square.

During the revolution, the square was baptized place de la Révolution, and the statue of Louis XV was torn down. A guillotine was installed about where the statue to Brest stands now. From 1793 to 1795, 1,343 people were beheaded here—Louis XVI, Marie Antoinette, Mme du Barry, Charlotte Corday (Marat's murderer), Danton, Robespierre, and Alexandre de Beauharnais (Joséphine Bonaparte's first husband) among them. A public execution always drew a massive audience, packing the square with eager onlookers for each of these grisly events.

After the Reign of Terror, in hopes of peace, the square was renamed place de la Concorde. A noncontroversial centerpiece was selected for it: the 3,300-year-old obelisk that was a gift from the viceroy of Egypt to Charles X in 1829. The obelisk is flanked by two fountains built from 1836 to 1846 recalling the fountains in St. Peter's Square in Rome. The north fountain represents river navigation, while the south fountain represents maritime navigation. Surrounding the square are eight statues representing the great cities of France: Bordeaux, Nantes, Lyon, Marseilles, Rouen, Brest, Lille, and Strasbourg.

As you cross **pont de la Concorde** toward the gleaming Palais Bourbon, be aware that you're walking on the stones of the Bastille, which were used in the construction of the bridge. Like the square it prolongs, the bridge changed names according to the political winds. First it was pont Louis XVI, then pont de la Révolution, then pont de la Concorde, then pont Louis XVI again before finally returning to pont de la Concorde.

When you cross the bridge, you'll be right in front of the colonnaded:

2. **Palais Bourbon and Assemblée Nationale.** The palace was built between 1722 and 1728 for the duchesse de Bourbon, the legitimized daughter of Louis XIV and his mistress, Mme de Montespan. The prince de Condé, the duchesse's grandson, embellished it in 1764 and added the adjoining Hôtel de Lassay. The palace was confiscated during the revolution and later rebuilt under the reign of Napoléon. In 1807, he commissioned Poyet to design a facade that would harmonize with the Roman-temple style of the Madeleine church. (If you look back across pont de la Concorde at the Madeleine, you can see that the palace and church are sister structures.) Since Napoléon, the palace has been almost continually used for official purposes and has housed the National Assembly since 1945.

There's a lot to look at on the decorated facade. Notice the 1842 Cortot pediment that represents France surrounded by Liberty and Order, with figures of Commerce, Agriculture, Peace, War, and Eloquence. The bas-relief on the right wing is by Rude and depicts Prometheus and the Arts. On the left is a representation of Public Education by Pradier. On top is a statue of Themis by Houdon on the right and Minerva by Roland on the left. The figures below are of Sully, Colbert, and other politicians.

The palace's interior is replete with sculpture and artwork. The Salle des Séances contains sculptures by Pradier, Desprez, Dumont, and Roman, as well as tapestries from Gobelins. The magnificent Bibliothèque is decorated with Delacroix paintings, and the grand Galerie des Fêtes links the palace to the Hôtel de Lassay. Guided inside visits are given free in French every Saturday at 10am and 2 and 3pm from the entrance at 33 bis quai d'Orsay. Get there 15 minutes in advance and bring a passport.

Walk left around the Assemblée Nationale (facing the building) to:

3. **Place du Palais-Bourbon,** with its dignified 18th-century mansions. The offices of *Vogue* are fashionably located at **no. 4,** and former president Paul Reynaud lived at **no. 5.** The statue in the center is of the Law, made by Feuchères in 1855.

Walk southward along **rue de Bourgogne.** Opened in 1907, this is one of the neighborhood's more commercial streets. Turn right at **rue de Grenelle** and at **nos. 138–140** on the corner is the:

4. **Hôtel de Noirmoutier.** This early-18th-century building is the headquarters of the Institut Géographique National. Marshall Foch, of World War I fame, lived here from 1919 until his death in 1929.

Return to rue de Bourgogne and continue south until it ends at **rue de Varenne.** Originally a rabbit warren *(garenne),* this street has been a prestigious address since the 18th century. Turn right and at **no. 77** is the:

5. **Musée Rodin,** housed in the Hôtel Biron. The works of France's greatest sculptor are beautifully displayed in this 18th-century mansion and garden. The hôtel's first owner was a highly successful wig maker, Abraham Peyrenc, but it was later occupied by a succession of more illustrious names, including Louis XIV's daughter-in-law. When Marshal Biron bought it in 1753, he gave glittering parties and opened the gardens to the public. An Italian cardinal and a Russian ambassador lived here until it was sold to Mme Sophie Barat, who turned the mansion into an exclusive convent. As Mother Superior, Mme Barat removed most of the ornamental woodwork, which explains the relative sobriety of the interior decoration. The convent dispersed in 1904, and the hôtel became a residence for artists and writers. Matisse, Jean Cocteau, Isadora Duncan, and Rainer Maria Rilke lived and worked in the mansion before Rodin moved here in 1910 at the height of his popularity.

In 1911, the French government bought the building and allowed Rodin to stay on condition that he leave his works to the state. The artist lived and worked here until his death in 1917, when the mansion was transformed into a museum containing an extraordinary collection of Rodin's greatest works, like *The Cathedral, The Kiss,* and *St. John the Baptist.* In the garden are *The Thinker, The Burghers of Calais,* and *The Gates of Hell.* For a nominal fee you can visit the delightful garden, with its outdoor cafe. The museum and garden are open Tuesday to Sunday: April to September 9:30am to 5:45pm and October to March 9:30am to 4:45pm. There's a separate admission fee for the museum.

After leaving the museum, cross rue de Bourgogne, continuing on rue de Varenne. The bland modern facade at **no. 78** conceals the:

6. **Hôtel de Villeroy,** a 1724 mansion that was built for Mme Desmares, an actress and model for the painter Watteau. Marshal Villeroy later bought the mansion, followed by the comte de Tessé and his wife. Thomas Jefferson frequently stayed as a guest of the comtesse, who shared his interest in politics and gardening. A few doors down and across the street at **no. 57** is the:

7. **Hôtel de Matignon.** *Matignon* is a meaningful and powerful word in France, for it's often used interchangeably with *prime minister,* whose official residence this has been since 1959. This noble residence was begun in 1721 by Jean Courtonne and was soon sold to Jacques Goyon de Matignon, comte de Thorigny. In the early 19th century, Talleyrand bought it; his dinner parties were so splendid that an entire new wing had to be added to serve as the dining hall. The Austro-Hungarian Embassy was here from 1884 to 1914. The house has the largest private garden in Paris, extending all the way south to rue de Babylone; Lionel Jospin lived here when he was prime minister from 1997 to 2002. Though the courtyard isn't open to the public, you can get a sense of the grandeur of this mansion through the large open portal.

A little farther on is the cul-de-sac Cité de Varenne, and almost next door at **no. 47** is the:

8. **Hôtel de Boisgelin.** Built by Jean-Sylvain Cartaud in 1787, this building is also known as Hôtel La Rochefoucauld-Doudeaubille and contains wood paneling from the Château de Bercy. It now houses the Italian Embassy.

Turn left on rue du Bac and right on rue de Grenelle to the:

9. **Fontaine des Quatre Saisons** near **nos. 57–59.** Like other parts of Paris in the 18th century, the faubourg St-Germain lacked an adequate water supply. When somebody complained, the answer was the construction of this fountain the size of a building. Sculpted by Bouchardon from 1739 to 1745, it's ornamented with allegorical figures of the City of Paris between the Seine and Marne rivers as well as sculptures of the Four Seasons and a bevy of cherubs.

Bouchardon anticipated the back-to-the-classics style of architecture that flourished later in the century. His ornate fountain was widely admired by everyone except Voltaire, who commented: "So much stone for so little water." **No. 59** is now a museum, the **Fondation Dina Vierny–Musée Maillol,** devoted to Catalan sculptor Aristide Maillol. It's open Wednesday to Monday 11am to 6pm, and there's an admission fee.

Walk back on:

10. **Rue de Grenelle,** crossing rue de Bac. On the left, **no. 73** is the **Hôtel de Gallifet,** where Talleyrand, as foreign minister, received Napoléon and Joséphine; **no. 75** is the **Hôtel de Furstemberg,** built for Count Egon de Furstemberg; and **no. 79** is the **Hôtel d'Estrées,** the residence of the Russian ambassador. Nicholas II and Alexandra stayed here in 1896. **No. 85** enjoys the rare distinction of having belonged to the same family, the d'Avrays, for 2 centuries. Notice the extraordinary **Hôtel de Bauffremont** next door at **no. 87.**

On the right at **no. 102,** the neoclassical **Hôtel de Maillebois** was built in 1660 but remodeled in 1750. It briefly passed into American hands when the revolutionary government awarded it as a National Lottery prize to American diplomat Edward Church. He sold it to a colleague, Fulwar Skipwith, who found the upkeep too high and quickly got rid of it.

At **nos. 104–106** was the Dames de Bellechasse convent, attended by Martha Jefferson, Thomas Jefferson's daughter. **No. 104** is now occupied by the Ministry of War Veterans, and the stately Louis XVI building at **no. 106** is a church. **No. 110,** the **Hôtel de Courteilles,** is notable for the 10 fluted Corinthian pilasters gracing the exterior. The Ministry of National Education occupies this 1778 building; as early as 1820 the Ministry of Public Instruction had been housed here.

Continuing in the direction of the river, turn right on:

11. **Rue de Bellechasse.** The name of this street roughly translates as "good hunting." When it was laid out in 1805, it halved the convent of the Dames de Bellechasse, who had adopted the name when they established themselves here at an ancient hunting lodge.

Turn right again on:

12. **Rue St-Dominique,** which took its name from a former Dominican monastery installed nearby. Painter Gustav Doré died at **no. 7,** where he lived with his mother. At **no. 5,** the 17th-century **Hôtel de Tavannes** has a handsome portal topped by a scallop and a pediment. In the 19th century it was the site of a noted literary salon run by Mme Svetchine, known as the "Russian Mme de Sévigné."

Make a left on boulevard St-Germain.

☕ **Take a Break** The lively **Mucha Café** serves copious salads and delicious lattes at 227 bd. St Germain.

After your break continue down the rue de Bellechasse. Then make a right on:

13. **Rue de l'Université.** Notice **no. 82,** where poet Lamartine died, and the attractive mansion at **no. 78,** built in 1687. **No. 51** is the magnificent **Hôtel Pozzo di Borgo,** also known as the **Hôtel de Soyécourt.** Behind the large portal flanked by Doric columns, the classically proportioned main building has pilasters that support a triangular pediment.

Turn left on:

14. **Rue de Poitiers.** In 1850, a monarchist group known as the Poitiers Street Committee used to meet at **no. 12, the Hôtel de Poulpry.** Painter Watteau decorated several rooms here very early in his career.

   At the end of the street, turn left on:

15. **Rue de Lille.** You'll pass several fine buildings on the left, including **no. 67,** the **Hôtel du Président-Duret,** built in 1706, and **no. 71,** the **Hôtel de Mouchy,** dating from 1775.

   On your right is the:

16. **Musée d'Orsay,** Paris's museum of 19th-century art. The Gare d'Orsay, a magnificent turn-of-the-century building, was one of Paris's main train stations. An iron-and-glass monument to the Industrial Age, it was constructed for the Compagnie des Chemins de Fer d'Orléans, which serviced France's southwest. By 1939, though, the tracks of the Gare d'Orsay proved too short for electric trains, and the station was virtually abandoned. Years later it was featured in Orson Welles's film version of Franz Kafka's *The Trial.* In the 1970s, it was classified as a historical monument and in 1986 became the "Impressionist Museum," designed by Gae Aulenti. The artistic riches are staggering—rooms full of masterpieces by pre-, post-, and neo-Impressionists including Manet, Monet, Degas, Renoir, and van Gogh. Lovers of Montmartre (see Walking Tour 6) will want to see Renoir's *Bal du Moulin de la Galette,* van Gogh's *La Guinguette,* Degas's *L'Absinthe,* and Toulouse-Lautrec's *Jane Avril Dansant,* all based on Montmartre scenes. The museum is open Tuesday, Wednesday, Friday, and Saturday 10am to 6pm; Thursday 10am to 9:45pm; and Sunday 9am to 6pm. From June 20 to September 20, the museum opens at 9am. There's an admission fee.

   Take a Break If you're up for a visit, drop by the museum's pleasant **cafe** before or after roaming the exhibits (entrance at 1 rue de Bellechasse).

   Directly opposite the museum is the:

17. **Palais de la Légion d'Honneur,** which boasts an eventful history. It was built in 1786 for the German prince of Salm, who so overextended himself in its construction that he then had to sell it to the architect to pay off the debt he had incurred. The prince continued to live in the mansion as a tenant until he ran afoul of the revolutionary tribunal, which dispatched him to the guillotine in 1794. The mansion was then seized and raffled off in the National Lottery. The winner was a wig maker who gave fabulous parties here—until he was sent to prison for forgery. Later, the Swedish ambassador made the mansion his residence, and Mme de Staël organized her famous salons here. Napoléon acquired the building in 1804 as the home for the Légion d'Honneur, which was to honor those "who by their talents contribute to the safety and prosperity of the nation." The Communards burned it nearly to the ground in 1871, but Légion members rebuilt the structure in 1878, following the original plans. The building now houses the **Musée de la Légion d'Honneur et Des Ordres de Chevalerie** with exhibits related to that prestigious decoration created by Napoléon (and still awarded today). The museum is open Tuesday to Sunday 2 to 5pm. There's an admission fee.

Continue in the same direction on rue de Lille, and at **no. 78** you'll come across the:

18. **Hôtel de Beauharnais,** the residence of the German ambassador. Also known as the Hôtel de Torcy, this building was constructed in 1713 by Germain Boffrand; it has some neo-Egyptian details, and John Russell has called it "the noblest of houses." Eugène de Beauharnais bought it in 1803. He was Napoléon's stepson, the son of Joséphine and Alexandre de Beauharnais, a nobleman from Martinique who fought in the American Revolution and embraced the French Revolution, only to die later by the guillotine (see Stop 1, earlier in this chapter). Eugène was named viceroy of Italy, and his sister Hortense married Louis Bonaparte, king of Holland, who was Napoléon's brother. In other words, Hortense was Napoléon's step-daughter—and his sister-in-law. She was also the mother of Napoléon III, who commissioned Baron Haussmann to redesign Paris.

Next door, at **no. 80,** is the:

19. **Hôtel de Seignelay.** Built in 1716, also by Germain Boffrand, it originally served as the residence of the marquis de Seignelay, grandson of Louis XIV's gifted finance minister, Jean-Baptiste Colbert. The duc de Charost was the next resident; this aristocrat was condemned to death by guillotine during the revolution, but saved from it by the intervention of his own peasants. The building now houses the Ministry of Foreign Trade.

The Palais Bourbon is just to the west, and so is the Assemblée Nationale Métro station, on the corner of boulevard St-Germain and rue de Lille.

Great Spots for Getting That Panoramic Shot

The roofscape of Paris is every photo-jockey's dream shot. You'll have to pay entrance fees for most places listed, but the price is small and the memory, and your photos, will last a lifetime. The highest lookout spot is the 276m (905-ft.) platform on the **Eiffel Tower.** The second-highest perch is the outdoor terrace on the 56th floor of the **Tour Montparnasse.** The **Grande Arche de la Défense** affords a magnificent view of the triumphal way designed by Le Nôtre in the 17th century, with its series of landmarks— the Arc de Triomphe, place de la Concorde, the Tuileries, and the cour Napoléon at the Louvre. Great views can also be had from **Sacré-Coeur** and the **Arc de Triomphe,** and don't forget the **tower of Notre-Dame.** Other less obvious spots include two department stores: **La Samaritaine** (usually free but temporarily closed for emergency renovations), which provides exceptional views of the Conciergerie, Notre-Dame, the Pont Neuf, and the Institut de France; and **Le Printemps** (free), which looks out over the Opéra and La Madeleine. There's a good view of the islands from the **Institut du Monde Arabe.** Breathtaking views can also be had from the *funiculaire,* run by Paris's urban transit system, that travels up the side of the Montmartre Butte in the 18e, and from the top of the **Centre Pompidou** (free).

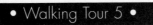
The St-Germain Quarter & Montparnasse

PART I FROM ST-GERMAIN-DES-PRES TO L'ODEON

Start: Church of St-Germain-des-Prés (Métro: St-Germain-des-Prés).

Finish: Carrefour de l'Odéon.

Time: 3 to 5 hours.

Best Time: During both equinoxes and at the winter solstice, when sunlight illuminates the cross at the St-Sulpice church.

Worst Time: Mondays or midafternoons, when Marché Buci is closed.

Since the early 1900s, odd-balls and artists have felt more at home in St-Germain than almost anywhere else in the world. The intellectual, argumentative, creative, and cosmopolitan spirit of the neighborhood has nurtured everyone from revolutionaries and painters to existentialists and jazz musicians. On this tour, you'll have the chance to sit in the same cafes where Hemingway, Sartre, and de Beauvoir once lingered. You can visit Delacroix's studio and museum. In the winding back streets you'll take in Henry Miller's favorite square, place de Furstemberg, and see where Sylvia Beach, Thomas Paine, George Sand, Hemingway, Picasso, and Stein and Toklas lived. Though the area has become overwhelmingly commercialized, especially along boulevard St-Germain, you'll find side streets crammed with art galleries and bookstores, small cinemas showing offbeat movies, and jazz clubs, theaters, cafes, and restaurants at all price levels. In fact, for two essential vacation activities—eating and shopping—there's no better place in Paris to visit.

The story of St-Germain began where that of so many other Parisian neighborhoods began—around an abbey. The church of St-Germain-des-Prés is on the site of the prosperous St-Germain abbey, which once owned much of the Left Bank. A village grew up around the abbey and began hosting the Foire St-Germain (St-Germain fair) in the 12th century. From the 15th to the 18th century, fairs held on the site of the Marché St-Germain attracted merchants and entertainers from all over Europe. The neighborhood's famous tolerance for diversity dates back to these gatherings.

In the late 18th century, the Odéon quarter became a hotbed of revolutionary activity. The main actors (save Robespierre) all lived in the area of carrefour de l'Odéon, where the statue of Danton now stands. They met in the Café le Procope, and Marat published revolutionary literature on cour du Commerce St-André; the first revolutionary massacre took place near the church of St-Germain-des-Prés.

As the political situation cooled down during the 19th century, the artistic soul of St-Germain slowly emerged. At the Ecole des Beaux-Arts, Delacroix and Ingres launched a revolution in painting that continued with Manet and the Impressionists. Artists who couldn't get into this prestigious school attended the Académie Jullian and set up their studios nearby.

The painters were followed by European poets and writers, who discovered that the neighborhood had everything

From St-Germain-des-Prés to l'Odéon

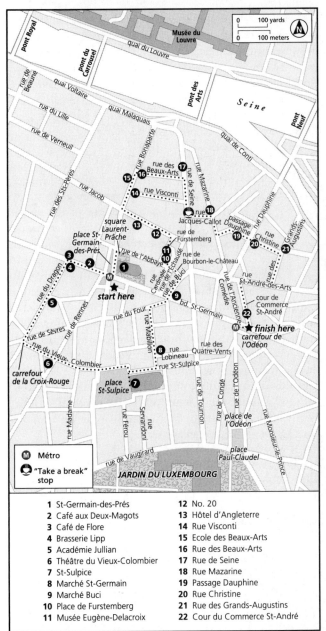

1 St-Germain-des-Prés
2 Café aux Deux-Magots
3 Café de Flore
4 Brasserie Lipp
5 Académie Jullian
6 Théâtre du Vieux-Colombier
7 St-Sulpice
8 Marché St-Germain
9 Marché Buci
10 Place de Furstemberg
11 Musée Eugène-Delacroix

12 No. 20
13 Hôtel d'Angleterre
14 Rue Visconti
15 Ecole des Beaux-Arts
16 Rue des Beaux-Arts
17 Rue de Seine
18 Rue Mazarine
19 Passage Dauphine
20 Rue Christine
21 Rue des Grands-Augustins
22 Cour du Commerce St-André

necessary for a literary life: stores to buy books, cafes in which to discuss them, and a climate that encouraged tolerance and freewheeling debate. André Gide published an avant-garde literary review, *La Nouvelle revue française,* and the poet Apollinaire took an apartment on boulevard St-Germain.

After World War I, American writers and journalists also began flocking to the Left Bank. Returning GIs who'd seen Paris wanted to know more about it, prompting many popular periodicals to open branch offices here. That brought jobs for English-speaking writers in Paris, and with a franc that was worth about 6¢ in 1921, life here was considerably cheaper than life in the United States. The American community straddled St-Germain-des-Prés and Montparnasse to the south. Writers moved between Gertrude Stein's apartment on rue de Fleurus and Sylvia Beach's Shakespeare and Company at 12 rue de l'Odéon.

When the Germans marched into Paris in 1940, the cultural life of the neighborhood came to a halt, only to rev up again with renewed energy after the war. The cafes along boulevard St-Germain, where Sartre and de Beauvoir came to write and keep warm during the winter, became the center of the quarter's social life. The famous couple drew legions of acolytes wanting to discuss the new philosophy of "existentialism," which examined the place of the individual in a godless universe. Picasso was another celebrated presence in these cafes, and his studio on rue des Grands-Augustins certified the area's growing vitality as an arts scene.

A new breed of Americans gravitated to the Left Bank in the postwar years. African-American jazz musicians like Sydney Bechet, Kenny Clarke, and Bud Powell found more tolerance and acceptance here than in their homelands, as well as a public ready to embrace their music. Authors Richard Wright and James Baldwin settled on the Left Bank, and beat writers Allen Ginsburg, Gregory Corso, and William Burroughs spent time here during the 1950s.

The residual glamour of those years made St-Germain one of Paris's most desirable residential districts—but also changed its character somewhat. Politicians and their relatives, newspeople, and actors all keep apartments here today. Philosopher Bernard-Henri Lévy, actress Catherine Deneuve, and newswoman Christiane Amanpour are some of the more celebrated current residents. Some say the recent opening of a

Cartier store on boulevard St-Germain marks the definitive end of an intellectual St-Germain; others point to the Christian Dior boutique that recently replaced the historic Le Divan bookstore as the coup de grâce.

The neighborhood really has come full circle from its days as host of the Foire St-Germain. The medieval idea of a fair to provide shopping and entertainment to foreigners and residents alike has been realized once again, while the clubs and cafes now have the added appeal of literary nostalgia. *Le plus ça change, le plus c'est la même chose.*

• • • • • • • • • • • • • • • •

Begin your walk at:

1. **St-Germain-des-Prés,** the oldest of the city's large churches. In Roman times, this area was an open field *(prés).* The original church was constructed in 452 as part of a monastery built by the Merovingian king Childebert to shelter relics he'd brought back from Spain. Childebert and other Merovingians were buried here, as well as the bishop of Paris, St. Germanus, for whom the church is named. In the 8th century, the abbey became part of the scholarly Benedictine order, but it was continually destroyed by the Normans, rebuilt, destroyed, rebuilt, and destroyed. In 1163, it was rebuilt for the last time. Throughout the Middle Ages, the abbey maintained its position as a wealthy and powerful intellectual center that answered directly to the Pope.

    In the late 18th century, French revolutionaries took over the abbey and filled it with titled prisoners. Later they held tribunals (very brief trials) that led to the massacre of more than 200 people, including a few of Louis XVI's ministers and his father confessor, in the abbey's courtyard (at the corner of rue Bonaparte and bd. St-Germain). After the massacre, while the bodies still lay in piles, there was an auction of the victims' belongings.

    The church's nave has murals by Hippolyte Flandrin (1809–64), one of Ingres's favorite students and winner of the 1830 Prix de Rome. You'll also find a memorial to 17th-century philosopher/mathematician René Descartes, whose skull is buried here; there's also a bust of Jean Mabillon (1623–1707), a French scholar and Benedictine monk who developed a technique for determining the authenticity of documents.

When you come out of St-Germain-des-Prés, turn to the right and walk around it to rue de l'Abbaye, in the rear. Behind the church is the tiny square Laurent-Prâche, a quiet park containing a **Picasso bronze bust of a woman** dedicated to Guillaume Apollinaire. Picasso and Apollinaire were great friends, and the bust was dedicated 41 years after Apollinaire's death.

Return to boulevard St-Germain and the "golden triangle" of the Café aux Deux Magots, Café de Flore, and Brasserie Lipp, all of which conjure up the prime years of St-Germain. The list of notables who frequented the cafes in the 1920s, 1930s, and 1940s includes just about everyone in Paris who put a pen to paper or a brush to canvas. Each cafe acquired its own following. In 1942, Sartre decided that Deux Magots was for old writers, Flore for young writers (such as himself), and Lipp for politicians. Now the distinctions are much more fluid, and most of the cafe habitués are likely to be tourists.

First on your right you'll see the:

2. **Café aux Deux Magots,** founded in 1881 and named after the wooden statues of two Chinese dignitaries *(magots)* sitting atop boxes of money attached to a column in the cafe. Journalist Albert Thibaudet described the cafe as "an intersection of roads, an intersection of professions, an intersection of ideas." The two terraces, one on boulevard St-Germain and the other facing the square in front of the St-Germain church, make this cafe ideal for people-watching. In the 1920s, it attracted the surrealists—like André Breton and Raymond Queneau—as well as Hemingway and Ford Maddox Ford. Janet Flanner, a close friend of Hemingway and the writer who (under the pen name Genêt) vividly captured Paris's 1920s cafe-and-salon scene, described Hemingway's habit of coming here to have "serious talk" and read works aloud. His love for Deux Magots is apparent in several passages of *The Sun Also Rises,* particularly the one in which Jake Barnes meets Lady Brett.

Next door the landmark bookstore **La Hune** played as important a role in literary Paris as the famous cafes. Founded in 1944 by a former philosophy student, the bookstore regularly exhibited modern artists and became a favorite haunt of Left Bank intellectuals.

Next is the:

3. **Café de Flore,** the oldest of the three cafes, founded in 1870. Pablo Picasso used to come here when he had his studio nearby on rue des Grands-Augustins. In the early 1940s, Jean-Paul Sartre and Simone de Beauvoir came here regularly to write, socialize, and drink coffee. De Beauvoir recalled afterward that she'd try to arrive early in the winter to get a seat next to the stove, where she'd write all day.

Across the street is the:

4. **Brasserie Lipp,** a favorite rendezvous since the 19th century. Politicians came for the *choucroute* (sauerkraut) served in the plush interior—the *choucroute* is still one of the best in Paris—and the brasserie later became a favorite watering hole of Saint-Exupéry and Camus. Today it attracts politicians, newspeople, and photogenic philosopher Bernard-Henri Lévy (known simply as BHL), who holds court downstairs, never (horrors!) upstairs.

From the Lipp, turn left on **rue du Dragon,** once named rue du Sépulchre. Its name was changed in the 18th century because residents preferred the name Dragon, after the huge gateway that had marked the entrance to cour du Dragon at **no. 7.** Proceed to **no. 31,** the:

5. **Académie Jullian.** Many artists who weren't accepted into the Ecole des Beaux-Arts attended this school, which opened in 1868 but didn't move to this location until 1890. In the French tradition, the academy was conservative and traditional, though considered inferior to the Beaux-Arts. Among the Americans who attended were Maurice Prendergast (1891–93), Max Weber (1905), and Jacques Lipchitz (1910). George Biddle described the place in 1911 as "a cold, filthy, uninviting firetrap." When he arrived, he found this scene: "Three nude girls were posing downstairs. The acrid smell of their bodies and the smell of the students mingled with that of turpentine and oil paint in the overheated, tobacco-laden air." He also said that while the artists worked "there was a pandemonium of songs, catcalls, whistling and recitations of a highly salacious and bawdy nature."

Continue down rue du Dragon to **no. 44,** where you can see a copy of the original ornamental dragon from which the street took its name.

You'll come to carrefour de la Croix-Rouge, dominated by a huge sculpture of a centaur by César. Turn left at the far end of the square onto **rue du Vieux-Colombier.** Influential poet/critic Boileau lived in a house on this street in the 17th century, and here he entertained Molière, Racine, and La Fontaine. Mme Récamier had a noted literary salon here later. But the highlight of the street is at **no. 21,** the historic:

6. **Théâtre du Vieux-Colombier.** Founded in 1913, the theater company intended to revive the classical tradition by focusing on the text, stripping scenery and design to a minimum. Undoubtedly the company produced its greatest success with the opening of Sartre's *No Exit* in 1943. Though the company's plays met with mixed results after World War II, the jazz club that opened in the basement in 1947 became an unqualified hit. Sydney Bechet and Claude Luter played New Orleans jazz at "le vieux-co," as it was called, while black-clad existentialists came from all over Paris to dance through the night. Saved from demolition in 1977, the building was named a historic monument in 1978 and purchased by the government. It's now back in business as a national theater supported by the government, with a repertoire that mixes classic plays and modern works.

At the end of the street, you'll come to:

7. **St-Sulpice,** one of Paris's largest and richest churches, with a splendid square around a fountain. Building began in 1646 but wasn't completed until the late 18th century; the south tower remains unfinished. The architects included Louis Le Vau and Jean-Baptiste Servandoni. As you enter St-Sulpice, note the enormous holy-water stoups made of natural shells, with intricately carved pedestals by J. P. Pigalle. Go right after you enter and you'll come across three of Eugène Delacroix's greatest masterpieces: *Jacob Wrestling with the Angel, Heliodorus Driven from the Temple,* and *St. Michael Vanquishing the Devil,* all completed in 1881. Wander through and view the other spectacular pieces of art.

Another interesting feature is the bronze **meridian line** running along the north–south transept. During both equinoxes and at the winter solstice (at midday), sunlight hits the line, runs along the floor, climbs up the obelisk to the globe on top, and lights the cross.

When you leave the church, head right along rue St-Sulpice and then turn left on rue Mabillon. On your right you'll see the shopping center:

8. **Marché St-Germain,** on the site of the Foire St-Germain. Though fairs *(foires)* had been held on this spot since the 12th century, in 1482 the monks of the St-Germain abbey built a permanent complex for the increasingly popular events. In addition to merchants selling their goods, there were games, shows, and novelty acts. Tailors rubbed shoulders with counts, and even the king attended regularly. A fire destroyed the marketplace in 1762, and the fair was ultimately discontinued; but the free-wheeling tradition of song and theater gave the neighborhood its character as the cultural hub of Paris. For many years, the Marché St-Germain was a renowned food market; it was recently redesigned, and the food market now occupies only a small portion of the modern mall. Stores are open Monday to Saturday 10am to 7pm.

Continue up rue Mabillon to **rue du Four.** When the St-Germain abbey controlled the neighborhood, the street was the site of the public oven *(four)*, where people came to bake their bread. In the postwar heyday of existentialism, the street was known for its many cheap cafes and hotels, but today impecunious philosophers will find little here within their budgets.

Turn right on rue du Four and follow it to boulevard St-Germain. Directly across the street is the:

9. **Marché Buci,** one of the city's liveliest markets. Here you'll find stalls selling fish, flowers, cheese, and fruit, as well as shop windows filled with mouthwatering pastries—the profusion of sights and smells will make you giddy. Be aware that if you arrive at lunchtime you won't find a market—it goes to lunch. The best time to arrive is between 9am and 1pm or later in the afternoon, until 7pm.

Turn left on rue de Bourbon-le-Château and cross rue de l'Echaudé onto rue Cardinale, which has changed little since its opening in 1700. Turning right will bring you to:

10. **Place de Furstemberg,** named for Cardinal Egon von Furstemberg, abbot of St-Germain-des-Prés in the late 17th century. It would be hard to find a lovelier and more tranquil hideaway. Here's how Henry Miller described it, though, in *Tropic of Cancer:* "Pass the Square de Furstemberg. Looks different now, at high noon. The other night when I passed by it was deserted, bleak, spectral. In the middle of the square four black trees that have not yet begun to blossom. Intellectual trees, nourished by the paving stones. Like T. S. Eliot's verse."

In May, Eliot's "intellectual trees" bloom and exude a sweet vanilla fragrance. Diagonally to the left across the square at **no. 6** is the:

11. **Musée Eugène-Delacroix,** the home and studio of the French Romantic painter (1798–1863) from December 28, 1857, to August 13, 1863. Here's an entry from his journal after he moved into this studio:

> Woke up the next morning and saw the most gracious sunlight on the houses opposite my window. The sight of my little garden and the smiling aspect of my studio always cause a feeling of pleasure in me.

Today, from inside the museum you can look out on the garden he describes.

The museum's holdings include Delacroix's portraits of George Sand, self-portraits, and animal paintings, plus the artist's collections of sketches and many letters. Exhibits rotate, so there's no telling which part of the enormous collection you're going to see. The museum is open Wednesday to Monday 9:45am to noon and 1:30 to 5pm.

After exiting the museum, go left up rue de Furstemberg to rue Jacob. (Note as you approach rue Jacob that there are some wonderful **fabric shops** to your left and right.) Go left on rue Jacob to:

12. **No. 20,** the former residence of Natalie Clifford Barney (1876–1972), who moved here from the United States in

1909 as a student and stayed for more than 60 years. Though virtually unknown in America, Barney was famous all over Paris for her literary salons. Virgil Thomson, Carl van Vechten, Sherwood Anderson, T. S. Eliot, James Joyce, and Marcel Proust were among the many who visited her Friday-night salon.

13. At **no. 44** is the Hotel d'Angleterre, which used to be the British Embassy in the 19th century. It's now a charming three-star hotel. Hemingway lived here for a time in the 1920s.

    Continue up rue Jacob to rue Bonaparte. Turn right on rue Bonaparte and make a quick right onto the narrow alley:

14. **Rue Visconti.** In 1962, the artist Christo blocked off the street with stacked oil barrels, calling the exhibit the "Iron Curtain." On your left at **nos. 20–24** is the residence where classical playwright Jean Racine (b. 1639) died on April 21, 1699. Educated at the Port-Royal abbey, he was Louis XIV's court dramatist and has been described as the most French of French writers. He's particularly well-known for the psychological realism of his characters.

    Just a bit farther on, **no. 17** was once the site of Balzac's print shop—yet another failed business scheme for the perpetually indebted writer—and where Delacroix had a studio for 8 years.

    Retrace your steps to rue Bonaparte. Turn right and head to **no. 14,** the:

15. **Ecole des Beaux-Arts,** the most famous of art schools, housed in a group of buildings from the 17th to the 19th century. The Beaux-Arts opened in 1648 as the Académie Royale de Peintre et de Sculpture, then became an individual institution in 1795. The Prix de Rome was bestowed by the Ecole des Beaux-Arts; its teachings remained traditional until well after World War II, and the entrance exam was so difficult—or perhaps so irrelevant—that even Rodin failed it. Among those who passed were Degas, Matisse, Monet, and Renoir.

    Continue up rue Bonaparte and turn right onto:

16. **Rue des Beaux-Arts.** At **no. 13** is the discreetly elegant L'Hôtel, where Oscar Wilde, broke and in despair, died in

1900. "I'm dying beyond my means," the English playwright/author wrote—and he was only paying 80 francs (12€/$15) a month for his room. Thomas Wolfe took up residence in the hotel in 1925 and wrote about it in his semiautobiographical novel *Of Time and the River.* Argentine writer Jorge Luis Borges also stayed here.

Painter Jean-Baptiste Corot had a studio at **no. 11,** where he welcomed Prosper Merimée, the author of *Carmen.* Fantin-Latour had a studio in **no. 8,** where James Whistler was a frequent visitor.

Make another right when you get to:

17. **Rue de Seine.** Look to your left at **no. 31,** the house of several who made unusual fashion statements. The female writer George Sand (see Stop 7 in Part II, later in this chapter) lived here and scandalized Paris by wearing pants. Raymond Duncan, brother of Isadora, lectured on Greek art and philosophy—clad in a toga and sandals and crowned in a laurel wreath. At **no. 33** is the art bookstore **Fischbacher Livres d'Art,** which stocks a fine selection of books on all genres of art, in both French and English. On the right (at the corner of rue Visconti) at **no. 26,** notice the sign of a famous 17th-century nightclub, Le Petit Maure.

Take a Break   At the corner of rue Jacques-Callot you may wish to stop at **La Palette,** a delightful terrace cafe that has been an artists' hangout since it opened in 1903. The interior is decorated with colorful murals, and a palette hangs over the bar. Note that the cafe is closed in August.

Then continue on rue Jacques-Callot to:

18. **Rue Mazarine.** Take a look at **no. 42,** to your left. Formerly a tennis court, it was converted into the Théâtre Guénégaud by Pierre Perrin to present his opera *Pomone,* the first opera presented in France. It later became the home of Molière's theater troupe.

Cross the street and turn right down rue Mazarine. Look for the entrance to the:

19. **Passage Dauphine** on the left, next to the parking garage. Ring the green button marked PORTE and enter

the gate. This winding passageway is an easy and scenic way to get from rue Mazarine to rue Dauphine.

Cross rue Dauphine and head directly into:

20. **Rue Christine,** opened in 1607. On the corner you'll see the **Hôtel d'Aubusson,** which once housed one of the hottest clubs in postwar Paris, Le Tabou. American jazz hit liberated Paris in the late 1940s and was quickly embraced by a war-weary public. A favorite party spot for singer Juliette Greco, Le Tabou attracted all the young existentialists, including, on occasion, Jean-Paul Sartre.

    Continue along rue Christine. In 1938, Alice B. Toklas and Gertrude Stein moved into an apartment at **no. 5** from one at 27 rue de Fleurus. They moved out during the Nazi occupation, but returned immediately after the liberation. Paris was full of American soldiers, and Stein plied them with whisky and cake and listened to their stories. By this time, her reputation as a writer and an art collector was firmly established. On a visit to deliver a housewarming bouquet, Janet Flanner was asked to make an inventory of Stein's incredible art collection. She found more than 130 canvases, 25 of them by Picasso. Stein died in 1946, but Alice B. Toklas lived here until 1964.

    As you continue along rue Christine, you'll find yourself on:

21. **Rue des Grands-Augustins.** At the corner, the restaurant **Jacques Cagna** ranks as one of the finest in Paris. Diagonally across the street, to the left (just a few steps up the street in the direction of the river), is **no. 7,** where Picasso lived from 1936 to 1955 near his good friend Gertrude Stein. Here he painted the masterpiece *Guernica* in 1937, as is duly noted on a plaque.

    Go right down rue des Grands-Augustins to **rue St-André-des-Arts,** then turn right to **no. 46,** where e.e. cummings lived in 1923. Continue along, looking for Bar Mazet on your left. Near the bar, go left onto:

22. **Cour du Commerce St-André,** a passage built in 1776 and strongly associated with the French Revolution. At **no. 9,** Dr. Guillotin perfected his little invention on sheep—before deciding it was fit to use on humans. This was also the site of the **printing shop** to which Jean-Paul

Marat (1743–93), Swiss-born revolutionary, would walk in his bathrobe every day to correct the proofs of *L'Ami du peuple,* the paper he founded.

You'll also find the rear entrance to **Le Procope** (formerly Café le Procope), founded by a Sicilian named Procopio just after the 1689 opening of the Comédie-Française (which used to be across the street). It quickly became the favorite of artists, writers, and playwrights. Beaumarchais waited in the cafe to hear the public's verdict after the opening of *Marriage of Figaro* at the nearby Théâtre de l'Odéon. Voltaire, Diderot, and Rousseau also gathered here, and the revolutionaries Danton, Marat, and Desmoulins liked this back entrance to the cafe; here they planned strategy around the tables. Later patrons included Benjamin Franklin, Victor Hugo, and Balzac. The main entrance is around the corner at **no. 1 rue de l'Ancienne-Comédie.**

Exit cour du Commerce St-André onto boulevard St-Germain. The little island at the center of the boulevard is carrefour de l'Odéon. The first part of the St-Germain tour ends here. If you don't wish to continue with Part II, the Odéon Métro station is right here. If you choose to continue, Part II begins where you're now standing.

PART II   FROM L'ODEON TO MONTPARNASSE

Start: Carrefour de l'Odéon (Métro: Odéon).

Finish: Cimetière de Montparnasse.

Time: 3 to 4 hours.

Best Time: Any time during the day.

Worst Time: In winter, when the Jardin du Luxembourg is bare.

This part of the walk first takes you through the Odéon section of the St-Germain neighborhood, which flourished after the Théâtre de l'Odéon was built between 1779 and 1782. Because of this district's proximity to the Latin Quarter and the print shops along rue St-Jacques, bookstores and publishers have a long presence

From l'Odéon to Montparnasse

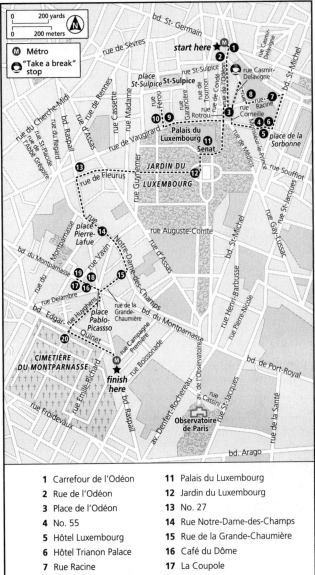

1 Carrefour de l'Odéon	**11** Palais du Luxembourg
2 Rue de l'Odéon	**12** Jardin du Luxembourg
3 Place de l'Odéon	**13** No. 27
4 No. 55	**14** Rue Notre-Dame-des-Champs
5 Hôtel Luxembourg	**15** Rue de la Grande-Chaumière
6 Hôtel Trianon Palace	**16** Café du Dôme
7 Rue Racine	**17** La Coupole
8 Rue Monsieur-le-Prince	**18** La Rotonde
9 No. 42	**19** Le Sélect
10 Rue Férou	**20** Cimetière du Montparnasse

here. Bookstalls were licensed to operate in the arcades around the Théâtre de l'Odéon in the mid–19th century. One of them expanded into the renowned publishing house Flammarion, which still has its headquarters on rue Racine.

Adrienne Monnier founded a bookstore, La Maison des Amis des Livres, on rue de l'Odéon in 1915, and it supported such talents as André Gide and Paul Valéry. Soon after, her friend/lover Sylvia Beach started Shakespeare and Company a few doors away. You'll pass by the site of both bookshops, as well as the former residences of Gertrude Stein, William Faulkner, and Richard Wright.

After relaxing in the Jardin du Luxembourg, you'll walk south to Montparnasse, a neighborhood that was another favorite haunt of artists and writers. In the 17th century, students from the Latin Quarter gathered here to read poetry and named the area Mount Parnassus after the Greek mountain consecrated to Apollo and the Muses. Cafes, dance halls, and theaters sprang up in turn-of-the-century Montparnasse, eventually luring artists from the increasingly touristy Montmartre. Before World War I, Chagall, Matisse, Picasso, Modigliani, and Max Jacob sipped absinthe in La Rotonde and Café du Dome with Russian exiles, who included Lenin, Trotsky, and Stravinsky. The scene picked up again in the 1920s with the opening of La Coupole and the addition of the American literary crowd—Hemingway, Dos Passos, Fitzgerald, and Miller.

The famous old cafes still draw a mix of Left Bank oldtimers and tourists, but the rest of Montparnasse has changed dramatically. This walk avoids the garish neon-lit neighborhood that emerged around the Tour Montparnasse when the 688-foot tower opened in 1967. Unlike other controversial architectural ventures that the public grew to accept, this looming monstrosity is as despised now as it was 30 years ago.

Instead, your walk will take you to the more interesting area east of the tower, where you can imagine the Montparnasse that attracted some of the most original minds of the 20th century. You can pay homage to the neighborhood's grand heritage in the Montparnasse cemetery at the end of the walk.

• • • • • • • • • • • • • • •

As I mentioned earlier in Part I of this tour, the little island in the center of boulevard St-Germain is:

1. **Carrefour de l'Odéon.** Take a look at the **bronze statue of Georges-Jacques Danton** (1759–94), one of the French Revolution's moderate leaders. A lawyer by trade, he became a leader of the Cordeliers and participated in the August 1792 storming of the Tuileries and subsequent overthrow of the king. After the revolution, he served as a member of the Assemblée National, but not for long—he was executed by his archrival, Robespierre, during the Reign of Terror.

    Continue across the street into:

2. **Rue de l'Odéon.** At **no.** 7 is the Galerie Régine-Lussan, but it was formerly Adrienne Monnier's bookstore, La Maison des Amis des Livres, a gathering place for French writers in the 1920s. Guillaume Apollinaire, Paul Claudel, Paul Valéry (whom Monnier actually published), and André Gide were frequent visitors. Monnier, who was Sylvia Beach's lover, committed suicide in 1955.

    A bit farther along on the right is **no. 10,** where Thomas Paine lived from 1797 to 1802 after his imprisonment by the revolutionary Tribunal.

    No. 12 is the site of Sylvia Beach's original Shakespeare and Company bookstore (1921–40). The store was first located on rue Dupuytren, but Sylvia Beach moved it here in 1921, just in time to catch the wave of expatriate writers rolling into Paris. Her store was a combination lending library, literary clubhouse, post office, and bank for Hemingway, John Dos Passos, Ezra Pound, Thornton Wilder, Gertrude Stein, F. Scott Fitzgerald, and others.

    Perhaps her most important contribution was her decision to publish James Joyce's *Ulysses,* a book considered so obscene that English typesetters refused to set type for it. Beach arranged for it to be printed in Dijon by Frenchmen unaware of what the words meant. "As the publisher of *Ulysses* Miss Beach became both martyr and heroine when its detractors and admirers began congregating, over the years, in her shop," wrote Janet Flanner some years after. Later, Bennet Cerf at Random House published the book and is reported to have made at least $1 million. Joyce received a $45,000 advance, but Beach never saw any money at all—even though she discovered, edited, and published the original work. She claimed not to mind and said she'd do anything for Joyce and his art. (Joyce never returned her favors, and when her shop was threatened with closure it was André Gide who rode to her rescue.)

Just a couple of doors down at **no. 18** was the building in which Adrienne Monnier and Sylvia Beach shared an apartment until 1937.

Continue to the semicircular:

3. **Place de l'Odéon,** a calm and elegant square dominated by the neoclassical **Théâtre de l'Odéon,** built in 1782 by architects Peyre and de Wailly to house the Comédie-Française. With nearly 2,000 seats, it was Paris's biggest theater at the time. Beaumarchais's groundbreaking *Marriage of Figaro* was both created and performed here in 1784. His hilarious story of cunning servants outwitting their thick-headed master expressed the democratic sentiments sweeping through Paris. As one commentator pointed out, Beaumarchais's predecessors "had always had the intention of making the great laugh at the expense of the small; here, the lowly could laugh at the expense of the great and the number of those ordinary people being so considerable one should not be astonished at the huge throng of spectators from every walk of life summoned by Figaro."

Turning to your left, you'll see at **no. 1** the building that used to house the Café Voltaire, a literary and artistic hot spot for 150 years. First frequented by Gauguin, Verlaine, Rimbaud, Whistler, and Rodin, this celebrated cafe attracted the "lost generation" in the 1920s. At **no. 6** is the **Hôtel Michelet Odéon.** Sherwood Anderson took a room here in 1926 and American poet Allen Tate (1899–1979) stayed here in 1929. He, too, was introduced to Ernest Hemingway by Sylvia Beach.

Bear left around the theater and walk straight through on rue Corneille to rue de Vaugirard. Turn left on rue de Vaugirard and walk to rue Monsieur-le-Prince, then go left to:

4. **No. 55,** on the right corner. Oliver Wendell Holmes (1809–94) lived here from 1833 to 1835 while studying medicine. A graduate of Harvard University, Holmes was a doctor, an occasional poet, and quite a wit. He came to this city to study because during his lifetime Paris was one

of the world's greatest scientific and medical centers. In 1857, he founded the *Atlantic Monthly* with James Russell Lowell. Dr. Holmes was easily flattered, and in his old age he took advantage of his hearing problems and would say to admirers, "I am a trifle deaf, you know. Do you mind repeating that a little louder?"

Return to rue de Vaugirard, turning right. At **no. 4** is the:

5. **Hôtel Luxembourg** (formerly the Hôtel Lisbonne), where author William Shirer lived in September 1925. It was a bargain at $10 per month, but Shirer reported that he had to use the bidet as a bathtub since the owner used the only bathtub as a coal bin. Further, he and other Americans who were accustomed to creature comforts had a lot of trouble learning how to use the hotel's pit toilets.

Retrace your steps, heading downhill on rue de Vaugirard. On the right at **no. 1 bis** is the:

6. **Hôtel Trianon Palace,** where Richard Wright took up residence when he first arrived in Paris in 1946 after a long battle for a passport with the U.S. government.

Turn left on **boulevard St-Michel.** At **no. 38** is the apartment Richard Wright sublet in 1946 from a professor who was on leave in Australia.

Continue and make a left on:

7. **Rue Racine** and head to **no. 3,** where George Sand rented an apartment in 1860, when she was 56 years old. It was her eighth residence in Paris. The building is now a Belgian restaurant with a sparkling Belle Epoque interior. Henry Wadsworth Longfellow lived at **no. 5** while studying at the Sorbonne. When he began his studies in 1826, he lived in a *pension de famille* (boardinghouse) until he began to feel imprisoned by the curfew and mealtime restrictions; he moved here so that he could be more independent.

Turn right on:

8. **Rue Monsieur-le-Prince.** At **no. 22** is the building in which American painter James Abbott McNeill Whistler had a second-floor studio. Many of his contemporaries disliked him because he had such a high opinion of himself. In fact, a wealthy man once visited here (when

Whistler was still virtually unknown) and inquired as to the total price of everything in the studio. Whistler quoted him a price of $4 million. As you can imagine, the man could hardly believe his ears. "What?" he exclaimed, to which Whistler replied, "My posthumous prices." This was probably the first and last time he ever underestimated himself.

Continue to **no. 14,** where in March 1959 Martin Luther King, Jr., visited Richard Wright in his third-floor apartment. Sylvia Beach's bookstore was near here, and she and Wright became close friends. She said of him, "Of all writers I have known, he is the most unselfish and thoughtful. In fact, none of the others . . . were interested in anyone but themselves. Fellas like Hemingway appear uncouth beside Dick Wright."

Take a Break   At **no. 12** rue Monsieur-le-Prince is **Chez Maître Paul,** a lovely little restaurant in which to stop for lunch. The chef is best known for his variety of wine sauces. If you miss lunch here, consider coming back later for dinner—and call ℂ **01-43-54-74-59** to make reservations if you plan to do so.

After a pleasant lunch, return to place de l'Odéon via rue Casmir-Delavigne. This time bear right around the theater and turn right on rue de Vaugirard, heading to:

9. **No. 42,** where William Faulkner stayed for several months in 1925. He spent 55¢ a day for his hotel room and another 45¢ a day on his meals. He particularly enjoyed going across the street to the Jardin du Luxembourg, where he could sit and write in peace. He describes the gardens in his 1931 novel *Sanctuary:*

> *In the Luxembourg Gardens . . . the women sat knitting in shawls and even the men play-ing croquet played in coats and capes . . . the random shouts of children had that quality of autumn. . . . From beyond the circle with its spurious Greek balustrade, clotted with move-ment, filled with a gray light of the same color and texture as the water which the fountain played into the pool, came a steady crash of music.*

Continue on to:

10. **Rue Férou.** Man Ray lived at **no. 2** when he came back to Paris in 1951, and Hemingway lived at **no. 6** while working on *A Farewell to Arms*. Hemingway had just left his wife, Hadley, and child and moved in with Pauline Pfeiffer, his mistress. When asked why he did so, he replied, "Because I'm a bastard."

    Retrace your steps to rue de Vaugirard and turn left. Across from Faulkner's old place and directly behind the Théâtre de l'Odéon is the:

11. **Palais du Luxembourg,** built by Marie de Médici shortly after she was widowed by Henri IV's murder. She was never a tenant, however, because before it could be finished she was banished by her son, Louis XIII, for opposing Cardinal Richelieu. During the revolution, the palace was used as a prison. Thomas Paine was imprisoned here by the revolutionary Tribunal and escaped execution only because the jailer missed the fatal X marked on Paine's cell door. Currently the French Senate sits here. The palace is open only 1 day a month and the line is often very long.

    Beyond the palace is the:

12. **Jardin du Luxembourg,** the most Parisian of all the city's parks. The gardens are immaculately tended, with long gravel walks that are bordered by tall trees and classical statues. Young adults fill the tennis courts while elderly gentlemen play *boules* (similar to the Italian game bocce). There is a playground and puppet theater for kids: The **Marionettes du Luxembourg** perform Wednesday, Saturday, and Sunday afternoons and all major holidays (for show hours, call © **01-43-26-46-47**).

    Isadora Duncan used to come here at 5am to dance, and Hemingway claimed he used to strangle pigeons in the park and take them home for supper. As you enter the gardens, go straight until you reach the impressive **Médici Fountain** (1624) on your left. This is a glorious place to sit and relax away from the crowds that gather around the central ornamental lake. After some leisure time, go around the back side of the bandstand area (near the bd. St-Michel entrance) to find **Rodin's bust of Stendhal** and

François Sicard's sculpture of George Sand (1905). As you head for the other side of the gardens, look for the rose garden, the beehives, and the orchard. Try not to miss the **miniature Statue of Liberty,** just to the left of the rue Guynemer exit.

Exit at rue Guynemer and cross onto rue de Fleurus to:

13. **No. 27,** the former home of Gertrude Stein and Alice B. Toklas; a plaque marks the spot. This was their most important residence, the apartment in which Stein amassed her incredible modern art collection and held her famous salons. Hemingway and Fitzgerald visited regularly, as did Picasso, Matisse, and Gauguin. Stein helped guide the careers of more than a few of these writers and artists, and took credit for many of their successes. The art dealers and collectors of her time watched what she and her brother, Leo, bought and then purchased similar works too. She had the power to make or break almost any modern artist who walked through her door.

When you come to boulevard Raspail, turn left. In another block, at the Notre-Dame-des-Champs Métro station, the boulevard branches off to:

14. **Rue Notre-Dame-des-Champs** on the left. Presently, you'll come to **no. 70,** where in 1921 Ezra Pound and his wife, Dorothy, moved into an apartment overlooking the courtyard and garden. Though all his furniture was made out of boxes and various discarded items, the place was charming. It didn't matter that Pound was poverty-stricken: He loved to throw parties, and just about everyone who was anyone during the time he lived in Paris visited this apartment. Hemingway often spent time here boxing and writing with Pound.

Katherine Anne Porter (1890–1980) lived in the same apartment in 1934. She came to Europe on a Guggenheim grant and joined Sylvia Beach's Shakespeare and Company Library in 1933. Porter remained in Paris until 1936 and is acclaimed for her collection of short stories *Flowering Judas* (1930) and her novel *Ship of Fools* (1962).

Across the street on your left is **no. 73,** where painter John Singer Sargent (1856–1925) once shared a studio with Carroll Beckwith. Here he completed his first major commission, a portrait of playwright Edouard Pailleron.

An American born in Florence, Sargent came to work in Montparnasse in 1874 at the age of 18. Already highly skilled in life drawing, he was able to jump to the head of the class shortly after he joined; as a result, he spent some time as Duran's assistant. By 1878, Sargent was out working on his own.

A few steps farther is **no. 72,** on your right. A second-floor apartment in this building was Malvina Hoffman's (1887–1966) first studio, and its only running water came from a tap down the hall.

This is where Hoffman worked on her first commission: a bust of the American ambassador to France, Robert Bacon. While living here, she met Rodin and visited his studio. One day he asked her to pick out one of the sculptures displayed in his studio and study it carefully until he came back. Knowing this to be a test, Hoffman intensely studied the one she'd chosen. Rodin returned about 20 minutes later and took her to another room. He gave her some clay and instructed her to sculpt from memory the head she'd studied. He walked out, locked the door, then came back a while later to find that she'd done an excellent job. He proceeded to take her to lunch, and that's how she was accepted as his student.

Only 5 years after she began working with Rodin, Hoffman achieved national recognition for her *Pavlova La Gavotte* and *Bacchanale russe.* She's also responsible for the creation of the Hall of Man at Chicago's Field Museum.

Across the street is **no. 75,** the home of Alice B. Toklas and Harriet Levy. Toklas first came to Paris with her friend and fellow San Franciscan Levy, and they moved into an apartment here. In 1912, Levy moved back to the United States, though Toklas decided to stay and move in with Gertrude and Leo Stein (she'd been typing manuscript pages for Gertrude since her arrival). Though Leo moved to Italy in 1914, Toklas stayed—for 32 more years.

Turn right at the corner of:

15. **Rue de la Grande-Chaumière.** *Chaume* means "thatch" and refers to the thatch-roofed dance halls that occupied the street until the 18th century. In 1783, an Englishman and a local restaurateur teamed up and turned the dance halls into a two-story building surrounded by

terraces and gardens where people could dance and drink. La Grande Chaumière became one of the most popular places in 19th-century Paris. The polka was introduced here in 1845, and then the cancan and another dance called the *chahut*, which was thought so vulgar that it was forbidden. The doors finally closed in 1853.

At **no. 14 bis,** on your left, is the **Académie de la Grande-Chaumière,** the art school begun by Antoine Bourdelle. Paul Gauguin took an apartment at **no. 8** on his return from Tahiti in 1893. On the right side (now the Best Western Villa des Artistes), **no. 9** was once the **Hôtel Liberia,** the haunt of many artists and writers. Among them was Nathanael West (1903–40), an American novelist born Nathan Weinstein who moved to Paris in 1926 and lived here for 2 years. He was fascinated with the idea of the American dream, and his best-known work is *Miss Lonelyhearts* (1933). West worked as an editor for several magazines, and 2 years after the publication of *Miss Lonelyhearts* he moved to Hollywood to become a scriptwriter.

Sculptor Malvina Hoffman also took furnished rooms somewhere on this street, which around 1920 was fondly referred to as the "rabbit hutch." Hoffman described the sounds of rue de la Grande-Chaumière as a veritable cacophony of "the calls of the knife sharpeners and mattress makers, the pan pipes of vendors of goats while leading their bleating flocks."

At **no. 8,** on your left, is the old studio of Amedeo Modigliani (see Walking Tour 7, Stop 16).

At the end of the street, you'll come to place Pablo-Picasso, which is the intersection of boulevards Raspail and Montparnasse. Notice the controversial **bust of Balzac** by Rodin (it was controversial because Balzac is rendered "warts and all," when at the time all statues were typically more idealized). Turning right onto boulevard Montparnasse will bring you to "cafe corner." First on your left is the:

16. **Café du Dôme,** which opened in 1897 and was popular with Americans and other expatriates in the 1920s. Hemingway and Sinclair Lewis both frequented the Dôme. An inebriated Lewis was insulted one night here

and exacted his revenge several years later in a magazine article:

> *Among the other advantages of the Dôme, it is on a corner charmingly resembling Sixth Avenue at Eighth Street, and all the waiters understand Americanese, so that it is possible for the patrons to be highly expatriate without benefit of Berlitz. It is, in fact, the perfectly standardized place to which standardized rebels flee from the crushing standardization of America.*

Next door at **no. 102** is:

17. **La Coupole,** where Henry Miller used to come for his morning porridge. This cafe opened in December 1927 and became a favorite spot of Russian exiles and émigrés (including Leon Trotsky and Igor Stravinsky) both before and after the Bolshevik Revolution. It also hosted the area's artistic community, including Josephine Baker, Sartre, Matisse, and Kiki de Montparnasse and her lover, photographer Man Ray.

    The 12 columns inside were painted (in exchange for a meal) by, among others, Brancusi, Gris, Léger, Chagall, Soutine, and Delaunay; they're registered as a historic monument. Of all the cafes on the corner, La Coupole is the most continuously crowded and boisterous.

    Across the street at **nos. 103–105** is:

18. **La Rotonde** has been housed at **no. 105** since it opened in 1911. This was more than just a cafe. Stanton MacDonald Wright, an American painter who frequented La Rotonde, described it as "a gathering place of most American and German artists; André, the waiter there, lent the boys [the artists] money and treated many as a father would." He also said that the cafe at that time contained "a small zinc bar in a long narrow room with a terrace where [they] drank and warmed [themselves] at great porcelain stoves."

    Around 1924, La Rotonde had become popular enough to warrant expanding it next door to **no. 103.** Apollinaire, Max Jacob, Picasso, and Modigliani enjoyed spending time in the cafe and nightclub. There was an

Kiki de Montparnasse: A Queen but Not a Lady

Born illegitimate, Alice Prin (d. 1953) was raised by her grandmother in Burgundy. Her mother called her to Paris to work—first in a printing shop, then in a shoe factory, and finally in a florist's shop on rue Mouffetard, where she was discovered by a sculptor. So began her career as an artists' model, for which she adopted the name Kiki de Montparnasse. At age 14, after her mother disowned her, she became a nightclub dancer at Le Jockey (Montparnasse's first nightclub), sporting black hose and garters.

Kiki was a voluptuous, seductive nonconformist who would bare her breasts to anyone who'd pay her 3 francs (.45€/60¢). She's most closely associated with Montparnasse because she spent 20 years frequenting cafes du Dôme, Le Sélect, and La Rotonde. As she got older, her quality of life deteriorated, and she began abusing drugs and alcohol, which ultimately caused her death. Hemingway, who wrote the introduction to Kiki's memoirs, called her "a Queen," noting that that was "very different from being a lady."

artists' gallery on the premises as well; Edna St. Vincent Millay, the American Romantic poet, came here often during her 1922 visit.

Up the boulevard a block at **no. 99** is:

19. **Le Sélect.** This cafe, one of the most popular in Paris in the 1920s, was frequented by Ernest Hemingway, James Baldwin, and Joan Miró (1893–1983), among others.

It was here that Isadora Duncan held an impromptu demonstration supporting anarchists Sacco and Vanzetti, who had been convicted of murder and sentenced to death. A fight with another of Le Sélect's patrons, journalist Floyd Gibbons, over whether or not Sacco and Vanzetti's lives should be spared prompted her to lead a small march to the American embassy to protest their impending executions.

Return to place Pablo-Picasso and turn right on boulevard Raspail. Make another right on rue Huyghens, which will take you to the entrance of the:

20. **Cimetière du Montparnasse.** Be sure you go in the main entrance. This will be a brief tour of the cemetery, with directions for the general locations of grave sites that you might be interested in visiting. You can pick up a map of the graves in the office to the left of the main entrance.

As you enter, go directly to the graves of **Jean-Paul Sartre** (1905–80) and **Simone de Beauvoir** (1908–86), on the right side of the roadway. Sartre was an existentialist playwright/philosopher/novelist. During World War II, he was taken prisoner but escaped and became a Resistance leader. During the Occupation, he wrote *Being and Nothingness* (1943) and *No Exit* (1944). He declined the Nobel Prize in 1964. Simone de Beauvoir, Sartre's intimate friend and occasional lover, was an existentialist novelist and a teacher of philosophy, but she's probably best known for her analysis of women in *The Second Sex* (1950). Toward the end of her life she wrote *The Coming of Age* (1970), about the ways different cultures treat and respond to the elderly.

Continue straight ahead, past the graves, and turn left at avenue de l'Ouest. On your left you'll find the grave of **Chaim Soutine** (1894–1943). Born in Lithuania, Soutine arrived in France in 1913 and became one of the greatest contributors to the Ecole de Paris (a loose term combining those artists who participated in the dadaist, cubist, and surrealist movements). He isn't very well-known because he suffered from depression and a lack of self-confidence that kept him from showing his work, but many believe Soutine was a man of great genius. It's said that he often destroyed his paintings. Soutine preferred the work of the old masters to that of his contemporaries and particularly admired Rembrandt's *Flayed Ox.* In fact, Soutine's own *Side of Beef* (ca. 1925) was inspired by the old masters. A frequent slaughterhouse visitor, he once brought a carcass home to paint; when his neighbors called the police to complain about the smell, Soutine answered them with a discourse on the importance of art over sanitation.

After crossing avenue du Nord, you'll find on your left the grave of French symbolist poet/critic **Charles Baudelaire** (1821–67). Only one volume of Baudelaire's major work, *Les Fleurs du mal* (1857), was published in his lifetime, and it was met with great animosity. Once considered obscene, *Les Fleurs du mal* is now regarded a masterpiece.

Cross avenue Transversale and on your left you'll find the grave of **Tristan Tzara** (see Walking Tour 6, Part I, Stop 12). Farther ahead, on your right across allée Raffet, is the grave of **Emile Antoine Bourdelle.**

Turn around and go right on allée Raffet to avenue Principale, following it around the circle to the left and straight through to avenue du Nord. Turn right to the grave of troubled actress **Jean Seberg** (1938–79), who co-starred with Jean-Paul Belmondo in *Breathless,* Jean Luc Godard's innovative 1959 film. Next is the grave of French composer **Charles Camille Saint-Saëns** (1835–1921), who made his debut as a pianist at age 10. Only 3 years later, he entered the Paris Conservatory, and for 20 years he was the organist at the Madeleine church. Saint-Saëns disliked modern music, and his most famous work was the romantic opera *Samson et Dalila* (1877).

After viewing the grave of Saint-Saëns, you'll see the grave of Romanian sculptor **Constantin Brancusi** (1876–1957) on the left. Brancusi decided to come to Paris to work, and soon after his arrival Rodin invited him to work in his studio. Brancusi did the unthinkable—he declined the offer, saying wisely, "Nothing grows well in the shade of a big tree." An abstract sculptor, Brancusi was unafraid of controversy. He believed in the absolute sim-plification of form and liked working in metal, stone, and wood. Continue on avenue du Nord, cross rue Emile-Richard, and enter the little cemetery, taking the door on the left. You'll see a tomb ornamented by Brancusi's famous sculpture *The Kiss* (1908).

Return to rue Emile-Richard and turn left. Go left again at avenue Transversale and right on avenue Thierry. On your left you'll see the grave of **Capt. Alfred Dreyfus** (1859–1935), the Jewish officer falsely accused of passing secrets to the German government and sentenced to

Devil's Island. The Dreyfus Affair revealed an ugly strain of anti-Semitism in the French military, targeted by Emile Zola's impassioned article *J'accuse*. Dreyfus was eventually exonerated when it was revealed that the evidence against him had been fabricated.

Exit the cemetery by returning to rue Emile-Richard, turning right, and continuing straight ahead to the exit. Then make a right and proceed to the Raspail Métro station.

Nighttime Strolls in Paris

Don't underestimate the pleasure of walking around after sunset. When the monuments loom floodlit out of the dark, the city is spellbinding. Approaching the **Eiffel Tower** from the **Palais de Chaillot** and **place du Trocadéro,** across the Seine, or the **Ecole Militaire** and the **Champ de Mars,** is a memorable experience. **Notre-Dame** acquires a golden hue, as does the **Louvre**—the pyramid takes on an outlandish appearance. The **Marais** and **place des Vosges** anchor themselves more strongly in the 17th century after the sun sets. Crowds mill around **place de la Bastille** and wander the **Latin Quarter.** The **Champs-Elysées** glitters as it never does during the day, and the **Arc de Triomphe** becomes truly triumphant as streams of automobile lights careen around it.

Montmartre

PART I THE BUTTE

Start: Place des Abbesses (Métro: Abbesses).

Finish: Place des Abbesses.

Time: 3 to 4 hours, depending on how long you spend in churches and museums.

Best Time: On a clear day, to enjoy the panoramic view from Sacré-Coeur.

Worst Time: Sundays, when the hilltop streets are jammed with people.

Montmartre has become saddled with an undeserved reputation as a tourist trap mainly because place du Tertre has been completely taken over by tourists and marauding gangs of painters. As you move away from this epicenter of tackiness, however, you'll come to appreciate why this area attracted people with a professional eye for light, color, and composition. To see the Montmartre beloved by van Gogh, Renoir, Utrillo, and countless other artists, you must climb the steep steps lined with iron lamps and take in the sweeping panorama of sky and sun over Paris. Meander

Montmartre: The Butte

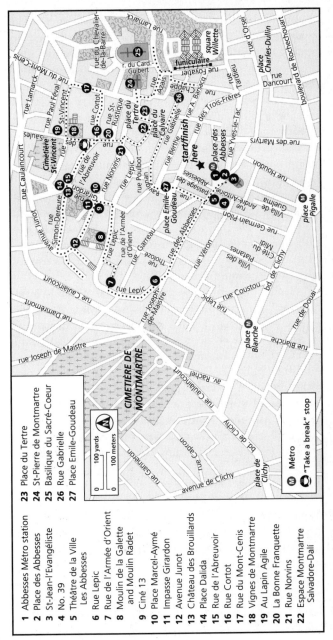

1 Abbesses Métro station
2 Place des Abbesses
3 St-Jean-l'Evangéliste
4 No. 39
5 Théâtre de la Ville
   Les Abbesses
6 Rue Lepic
7 Rue de l'Armée d'Orient
8 Moulin de la Galette
   and Moulin Radet
9 Ciné 13
10 Place Marcel-Aymé
11 Impasse Girardon
12 Avenue Junot
13 Château des Brouillards
14 Place Dalida
15 Rue de l'Abreuvoir
16 Rue Cortot
17 Rue du Mont-Cenis
18 Vignes de Montmartre
19 Au Lapin Agile
20 La Bonne Franquette
21 Rue Norvins
22 Espace Montmartre
   Salvadore-Dalí
23 Place du Tertre
24 St-Pierre de Montmartre
25 Basilique du Sacré-Coeur
26 Rue Gabrielle
27 Place Emile-Goudeau

Ⓜ Métro
☕ "Take a break" stop

0 100 yards
0 100 meters

through the lanes lined by foliage and whitewashed houses and suddenly you'll enter a country village that overlooks the bustling metropolis at its feet without quite being a part of it.

The Sacré-Coeur church on top of Montmartre is often the first monument visitors see as they come into Paris from Charles de Gaulle airport. It's not only the most conspicuous building in Paris, but also the largest building on the *butte* (hill) of Montmartre. The absence of other big buildings here isn't because developers wished to retain the rustic ambience of the village, but because the terrain isn't stable enough to withstand heavy weight. Since the time of the Romans, Montmartre has been heavily quarried for its supply of gypsum. Remember plaster of Paris? Until the 17th century, Montmartre supplied such a quantity of this construction material that it used to be said that "there's more of Montmartre in Paris than Paris in Montmartre." Though the quarries closed more than a century ago, a web of tunnels remains.

Besides quarrying gypsum in Montmartre, the Romans built the first temple on top of the hill and dedicated it to the Roman god Mercury. The hill was known at various times as mont de Mercure or mont de Mars (for the god Mars), until the early Christians named it mont des Martyrs for the martyrdom of St. Denis. The first bishop of Paris, Denis and two of his prelates, St. Rustique and St. Eleuthère, were arrested and beheaded at the top of the hill in the 3rd century. A miracle then happened: St. Denis is said to have picked up his own head and carried it to a nearby fountain, washed the blood from his face, and then walked 6.4km (4 miles) before he collapsed.

The religious importance of the hill led to the building of the St-Denis abbey, which was replaced by the royal Abbey of Montmartre in 1133. This powerful Benedictine abbey was funded by Louis VI and his wife, Adélaide, who finished her days there. The church, St-Pierre-de-Montmartre, is the only remaining part of this Benedictine order.

Like most medieval abbeys, the Abbey of Montmartre became involved in wine production, and before long the hilltop was covered with vineyards. In the 16th century, the first windmills appeared to press grapes and also to grind the grain produced by the surrounding villages. At one time there were 13 windmills gracing the hill. Only two remain: the Moulin de la Galette (Blute-Fin) and the Moulin Radet.

By the 18th century, Montmartre was a bustling village. Although not yet part of Paris, it supplied the capital with wheat, wine, and above all gypsum. Wine production gradually declined with increasing competition from the wines produced in the south of France. Now only a symbolic vineyard remains, providing more nostalgia than drinkable libations.

The gypsum quarries closed in 1860, the same year that Montmartre was annexed as part of Paris. The bucolic life on the hill was brutally interrupted by the Paris Commune of 1871. Cannons had been placed on top of Montmartre to defend the city against the Prussians, and when the government in Paris tried to remove them, people rioted and two generals were shot. The uprising spread throughout Paris before being suppressed after several weeks of bloodshed.

At the end of the 19th century, Montmartre became the scene of Paris's wildest nightlife. The Moulin Rouge, at the foot of the hill, was one of many cabarets along the lower boulevards that attracted anyone in search of a good time. While the aristocracy went to the opera, the windmills of Montmartre were converted into hugely popular dance halls where the atmosphere was anything but decorous.

Meanwhile, the picturesque streets and anything-goes Montmartre spirit began attracting a group of radical painters. In La Bonne Franquette and Au Lapin Agile on the Butte and innumerable clubs on boulevards de Clichy and de Rochechouart, Renoir, Manet, Picasso, Toulouse-Lautrec, van Gogh, and Utrillo gathered. Many of the painters had studios in and around the neighborhood; some, such as Renoir and Utrillo, portrayed the color and vivacity of Montmartre life in their paintings.

After World War I, Montmartre became too expensive, and artists moved on to Montparnasse. Today, the neighborhood is home to a number of people in the film and entertainment industries. The streets that had inspired a profusion of fine paintings were recently evoked in Woody Allen's musical, *Everyone Says I Love You*. When Allen's character wants to impress his lady love with his artistic soul, he moves to (where else?) Montmartre.

• • • • • • • • • • • • • • • • •

Begin your walk at the:

1. **Abbesses Métro station,** the deepest in the city at 35m (116 ft.) beneath street level. As you come up the stairs, you'll see a vast fresco of Montmartre scenes executed by local artists. Or you can take the elevator. You'll emerge from one of the two remaining Art Nouveau stations (the other is at Porte Dauphine) designed by Hector Guimard at the beginning of the 20th century. These imaginative entrances were designed to resemble a shell of swirling glass and iron that bridges the underworld and the street.

Once you reach the street you'll be on:

2. **Place des Abbesses,** the centerpiece of an unpretentious and slightly offbeat neighborhood that's still inexpensive enough to attract students and artists. Centuries earlier, this square marked the entrance to the Women's Abbey of Montmartre. In 1590, Henri de Navarre (later Henri IV, the Vert Galant) kept Paris under siege from his garrison on Montmartre hill, and handsome Henri seduced the head abbess, Claude de Beauvilliers. His example was swiftly followed by his lieutenants and other nuns. Word spread to the besieged Parisians, who began referring to the abbey as "the army's whorehouse on the hill." After the siege was lifted, the enamored Claude de Beauvilliers followed Henri to Senlis, where she introduced him to her German cousin, Gabrielle d'Estrées. Henri allegedly seduced the cousin and eventually gave Claude another abbey to run in recompense.

In front of the Métro station is:

3. **St-Jean-l'Evangéliste** (1904), the first church to be built entirely of reinforced concrete. The brick surface has given the church the nickname St-Jean-des-Briques, but the slenderness of its pillars and the graceful arches on the front make it a fine example of modern architecture. The floral motifs inside recall the Art Nouveau style, and the stained-glass windows were inspired by 16th-century German paintings.

When you leave the church, turn left. Go down the stairs on your left, and at the foot of rue André-Antoine is:

4. **No. 39,** the house where painter Georges Seurat died suddenly from diphtheria in 1891. The neoimpressionist

master moved here in 1890; this is where he painted *Le Chahut,* depicting a dance from a Montmartre music hall.

Return to the street. A few steps to the left of rue André-Antoine is the:

5. **Théâtre de la Ville Les Abbesses,** a city-subsidized theater redesigned in 1996 by Charles Vandenhove. The neoclassical brick-colored facade makes an interesting contrast with the adjacent St-Jean-l'Evangéliste church.

Continue up rue des Abbesses, a lively street of shops, boutiques, cafes, and restaurants. Notice the view of the windmill Moulin de la Galette as you pass rue Tholozé on the right (more about that below). A few steps farther, rue des Abbesses branches off into:

6. **Rue Lepic,** which climbs to the top of the Butte. Currently in a state of disrepair, **no. 54,** on the right, is the building in which Vincent van Gogh and his brother, Théo, lived from 1886 to 1888 on the third floor. Vincent and Théo had an extraordinarily strong relationship; Théo helped support Vincent, both financially and emotionally, throughout his life, particularly during his art career. Théo ran an art gallery, which at the time exhibited very traditional art, but he believed in his brother's talents.

The gardens and windmills of Montmartre inspired a number of van Gogh paintings. During his time in the studio, van Gogh became friendly with Toulouse-Lautrec, Gauguin, and Signac, under whose influence his palette became brighter and more colorful.

Continue along rue Lepic and turn right at:

7. **Rue de l'Armée d'Orient,** filled with turn-of-the-20th-century artists' studios. **No. 4** is the **Théâtre Montmartre-Galabru,** which used to present the works of students at the Renée Maubel conservatory. In 1917, the theater mounted Appollinaire's surrealist play *Les Mamelles de Tirésias,* which was later made into an opera by Poulenc.

Follow the street to rue Lepic and turn right. Presently you'll come to the last two windmills of Montmartre, the:

8. **Moulin de la Galette and Moulin Radet.** The first, at **no. 75,** is the **Moulin de la Galette,** originally called the Blute-Fin, built in 1622. Both windmills belonged to the Debray family in the 19th century. According to legend,

three Debray brothers were killed in 1814 defending their hill from the Russians. The fourth brother and his son hid in the windmill. When discovered, the father shot a Russian officer in the head. In retaliation, he was seized and cut into four pieces, each piece attached to a sail of the windmill. His widow had to collect his remains in a flour sack and bring them to the cemetery.

The son was wounded but recovered and in the 1860s transformed the windmill into a public dance hall called the Moulin de la Galette because it sold *galettes,* cakes made with the flour ground inside the windmills. Later on, the dance hall *(bal populaire)* was frequented by Toulouse-Lautrec, van Gogh, Utrillo, and Renoir, who portrayed it in the celebrated painting *Le Moulin de la Galette,* now in the Musée d'Orsay (see Walking Tour 4, Stop 16).

A few steps away at the corner of rue Lepic and rue Girardon, the second windmill, **Moulin Radet,** is now part of a restaurant.

Turn left on rue Girardon and head to its intersection with avenue Junot, where you'll find:

9. **Ciné 13,** a tiny art-house cinema. Immediately to the right facing the cinema is the gated entrance to a **private compound.** This compound is so private that the residents have chosen the names of famous artists as their aliases on the outside intercom. The panel of names reads like a who's who of French art—Degas, Matisse, Utrillo, Toulouse-Lautrec, and Seurat are some of the supposed tenants.

Diagonally across the street is:

10. **Place Marcel-Aymé,** named for writer Marcel Aymé, who lived in the building here until his death in 1967. The curious sculpture of a man emerging from a wall was executed by actor and Montmartre resident Jean Marais in 1989. "The Man Who Passed Through Walls" *(Passe-Muraille)* was a Montmartre character gifted with the ability to pass through walls. According to the story, he was a petty bureaucrat who first used his powers to annoy his boss and then progressed to various amusing escapades. Finally, after a night of passionate love, he was trapped in a wall. It's said that on certain restless nights, you can still hear his sad wails echoing through Montmartre. His exploits were dramatized in Marcel

Aymé's 1943 *Le Passe-Muraille,* which was subsequently made into a movie and a hit musical.

Across the street is the:

11. **Impasse Girardon,** which used to lead to the celebrated fontaine St-Denis, where St. Denis allegedly washed his decapitated head. Water from the ancient fountain was said to make young women faithful to their husbands. The fountain disappeared into a plaster quarry in 1810, and some say French marriages have gone downhill ever since.

    The impasse is bordered by the **square Suzanne-Buisson,** a lovely secluded park. A statue of St. Denis marks the spot of the former fountain and overlooks a *boules* court (similar to that of the Italian game, bocce) where there's often a game in progress.

    A number of artists have made this impasse their home, including sculptor Henri Laurens, Basque sculptor Paco Durrio, and expressionist painter Gen Paul.

    Continue along to:

12. **Avenue Junot,** a curving 20th-century street planted with linden trees. **No. 11,** on the left, is an artists' hamlet in which Maurice Utrillo (1883–1955) resided from 1926 to 1937. Son of the talented painter/circus acrobat Suzanne Valadon, Utrillo took up painting in 1902 in an unsuccessful attempt to curb his drinking problem. As he was born and bred in this neighborhood, his work centered on street scenes, especially of Montmartre. The originality and poetry of Utrillo's early vision was lost in later life, when he became more of a painting machine, turning out 4,000 canvases between 1920 and 1940. Nevertheless, he remains the painter most closely identified with Montmartre.

    No. 13 was the studio of another Montmartre artist, Francisque Poulbot (1899–1946), a designer known for his drawings of street urchins. His distinctive illustrations were widely copied and gave rise to the term *petits poulbots* to describe street urchins. Several of his designs ornament the top of the building.

    No. 15 was the home of Romanian-born French poet Tristan Tzara (1896–1963). He's best known as the founder of the dadaist movement. Tzara and André

Breton (1896–1966) collaborated briefly before Breton broke with the dadaists to found the surrealist movement. Adolf Loos, architect of Tzara's house, had a modernist's disdain for architectural ornamentation. "We have conquered ornament, we have finally made our way to the absence of ornamentation," he wrote. This appealed to Tzara's dadaist sensibilities, and he brought Loos to Paris from Vienna and commissioned him to build this house from cement and stone.

At **no. 23** is the unusual leafy passage, M18. A giant rock, known as *le rocher de la sorcière* ("The Witch's Rock"), is at the top of stairs leading down to rue Lepic.

Next at **no. 25** is the **Villa Léandre,** built in 1926. This short cul-de-sac of houses surrounded by creeping vines and tiny gardens proves that there'll always be an England—even in Montmartre. The style is so English that one house on the right even bears the sign 10 DOWNING STREET.

Return to avenue Junot, go down the hill a few steps, and turn right at rue Simon-Dereure. On the right ahead of you, you'll come to another entrance to the square Suzanne-Buisson, which once was the grounds of the:

13. **Château des Brouillards.** This 18th-century mansion fell into disrepair and became a sort of shelter for homeless, impoverished artists around 1890. It has been inhabited by the Casadesus family of musicians since 1928.

Take the stairs on the left that lead to the **allée des Brouillards.** One of the houses behind the foliage on the left was the studio and family residence of Pierre-Auguste Renoir from 1890 to 1897. His son, Jean, was born here in 1894 and went on to direct classic French films like *Rules of the Game* and *The Grand Illusion.*

At the end of the allée des Brouillards you'll arrive at:

14. **Place Dalida,** named after the French singer who lived nearby on rue d'Orchampt. She was born in 1933 in Cairo, and her striking looks and dusky alto made her immensely popular; she recorded more than 500 songs in eight languages and sold more than 100 million records. She committed suicide in 1987 after romantic disappointments.

Take the road opposite the allée des Brouillards, which is:

15. **Rue de l'Abreuvoir.** This leafy street was a country lane used by horses and cattle on their way to the watering trough *(abreuvoir)* that once stood on the site of **no. 15.** The Café de l'Abreuvoir, a former artists' hangout, was at **no. 14;** you can see a reconstruction of it in the Musée du Vieux Montmartre. Impressionist painter Camille Pissarro rented **no. 12** as a *pied-à-terre* between 1888 and 1892, while his family stayed in the countryside. Notice the sign of the eagle at **no. 4.** The house belonged to Henry Lachouque, the noted historian of Napoléon, whose symbol was an eagle. On the side, this ivy-covered cottage has a sundial with a picture of a rooster and the legend QUAND IV SONNERA, JE CHANTERAI ("when four sounds, I'll sing"). **No. 2** is the "little pink house" painted by Utrillo; it was his earliest success.

Take a Break At **no. 2** rue de l'Abreuvoir, Utrillo's subject is now **La Maison Rose.** The restaurant serves inexpensive crepes and a few other standard dishes, but the real attraction is the location. From an outside seat, you'll gaze across at the humble cottages draped in vines and shrubbery and begin to understand why artists fell in love with this neighborhood.

At the end of rue de l'Abreuvoir, cross rue des Saules and take a few steps to the right onto:

16. **Rue Cortot.** At **no. 12** is the **Musée du Vieux Montmartre.** This has been a beehive of artistic activity since 1875, when the 17th-century building was converted into artists' studios. In 1876, Renoir rented a studio in the left wing, where he put the finishing touches on *Le Moulin de la Galette.* In 1896, Suzanne Valadon moved into the first floor with her husband and son, Maurice Utrillo, who later had his own studio here. Fauvist Raoul Dufy moved into the right wing in 1901, and painter Emile Bernard entertained his friends Gauguin and van Gogh here.

Besides charting Montmartre's history in a series of exhibits, the museum features a re-creation of the workroom of Gustave Charpentier (composer of the opera *Louise*); a reconstruction of Café de l'Aubrevoir, another of Utrillo's favorite spots; and an entire room devoted to

Emile Bernard. The museum is open Tuesday to Sunday 11am to 6pm, and there's an admission fee.

No. 6 is the house where composer Erik Satie (1866–1925) lived in a tiny room he called his "closet." He earned his living banging out tunes in Montmartre cabarets, and in his spare time composed the haunting piano cycles *Les Sarabandes, Les Gymnopédies,* and *Les Gnossiennes.* Nicknamed "Esoteric Satie" because of his enthusiasm for matters supernatural, the composer had a love affair with his neighbor, Suzanne Valadon, and later contributed the music for the ballet *Parade,* created by Sergei Diaghilev.

At the end of rue Cortot is a water tower that has irrigated the neighborhood since 1927. Turn left on:

17. **Rue du Mont-Cenis** and go down the stairs. **No. 22,** at the corner of rue St-Vincent, is the site of a house rented by composer Hector Berlioz in 1834. Though the house was the subject of a painting by Utrillo, *La Maison de Berlioz,* it was torn down in 1926. When he and his wife moved into the residence, Berlioz wrote to his sister, "We have a little four-room apartment, a garden and a view of the plain of Saint-Denis for 70 francs a month. It is a lot less expensive . . . and in a half hour we are in Paris."

Turn left. A little way down the road is the:

18. **Vignes de Montmartre,** one of two remaining vineyards in Paris. The vineyard produces approximately 500 bottles of Clos Montmartre red annually. Every year on the first Saturday of October there's a celebration, the Vendanges, in honor of the harvest. If you're lucky enough to be in Paris at harvest time, you'll find it's quite a party—there's even a parade.

On your right is:

19. **Au Lapin Agile,** the original Cabaret des Assassins. Legend has it that the cabaret got its name because a band of assassins broke in and killed the owner's son. It was renamed in 1880 because of a sign featuring a rabbit *(lapin)* in a bow tie, painted by André Gill. People began saying that it was the Cabaret à Gill, which eventually became Agile.

The building originally belonged to a famous Parisian singer named Aristide Bruant, who gave it to Father Fred, who used to entertain his clientele by singing and playing the guitar. Since Montmartre was the heart of artistic Paris at the time, there was much discussion here about the "meaning of art." Popular writer Roland Dorgeles took it on himself to make a mockery of the debate by dipping the tail of Father Fred's donkey into some paint, smearing it on a canvas, and exhibiting the result, called *Le Coucher du soleil sur l'Adriatique (Sunset over the Adriatic)*. Much to Dorgeles's amusement, the critics actually liked it. Of course, he did eventually tell them (to the further amusement of many Parisians) that it was merely a joke.

Au Lapin Agile was often captured on canvas by Utrillo and is still active as a cabaret presenting traditional French songs. Today this corner is one of the most visited and photographed in all of Paris.

Go up rue des Saules. At the corner of rue St-Rustique is the restaurant:

20. **La Bonne Franquette,** which was another watering hole of the Impressionists: Pisarro, Sisley, Cézanne, Toulouse-Lautrec, Renoir, Monet, and writer Emile Zola all gathered here. Van Gogh painted the garden in 1886; his painting *La Guinguette* is in the Musée d'Orsay (see Walking Tour 4, Stop 16).

Turn right a few steps ahead onto:

21. **Rue Norvins,** the principal link between Montmartre and Paris from the 11th century. You'll come to **no. 22,** the country house known as **Folie Sandrin,** after its original 18th-century owner. In the first half of the 19th century, it was an insane asylum. The inmates included a man who wrote a 62-page book without using the letter a; a former lady-in-waiting to Marie Antoinette who went mad after failing to marry Robespierre; and writer Gérard de Nerval, who used to stroll the gardens of the Palais Royal with his pet lobster on a leash. The mansion now belongs to the city of Paris, which has turned it into an artists' residence.

Retrace your steps to the corner of rue Norvins, rue des Saules, and rue St-Rustique. This crossroads was frequently painted by Utrillo—though without the shops selling trinkets, postcards, and T-shirts. Go up rue Norvins a few feet and turn right on rue Poulbot. Follow the curve to **no. 11,** the:

22. **Espace Montmartre Salvadore-Dalí,** housing a permanent display of 330 works by the Spanish artist. The exhibit's darkness is punctuated by lights that move from one painting to another as Dalí's voice moves through the exhibit along with visitors. The experience, like the artist's works, is somewhat surreal. Also here are an art gallery and a library. The museum is open daily 10am to 6pm, and there's an admission fee.

When you come out of the museum, go left and up a few steps to place du Calvaire and enjoy the view over south Paris. Turn left and you'll come to:

23. **Place du Tertre,** one of the most frequented tourist spots in Paris, if not the world. Although it was once a typical 18th-century village square, it's now a place to eat mediocre, overpriced food surrounded by street artists clamoring to sketch your picture while some shady character picks your pocket.

Unless that sounds good to you, move on. Continue across the square to rue Norvins, where you'll make a right and arrive at the historic church of:

24. **St-Pierre de Montmartre,** probably built on the site of an early sanctuary to St-Denis, which replaced a Gallo-Roman temple. Consecrated in 1147, this church is one of the oldest in Paris, and it is, in fact, the last trace of the original Abbey of Montmartre. The chancel and the nave date from 1147, although the west facade through which you enter was reconstructed in the 18th century. In the left aisle is the tombstone of the founder of the abbey, Queen Adélaide, wife of Louis VI. The stained-glass windows date from 1954; earlier ones were destroyed by a bomb during World War II.

When you leave the church, head left along place du Tertre, go downhill, and take the first left, rue Azais, to:

25. **Basilique du Sacré-Coeur,** certainly one of Paris's most striking churches and probably the most controversial.

After the capitulation of Paris at the hands of the Prussians and the bloody 1871 uprising known as the Paris Commune, the archbishop of Paris wanted to build a church as an atonement for the "sins" of Parisians and as a reaffirmation of Christian faith. The top of Montmartre was chosen not only for its prominence but also because of its association with the martyrdom of St. Denis. The only problem was that the necessary land was privately owned. The church asked the National Assembly to expropriate the land, which raised protests from deputies who argued that the construction of a church was a religious and not a public undertaking and thus deserved no state support. The fact that the spot chosen was where the Communards first battled government forces was also deeply unpopular with deputies who had sympathized with the left-wing uprising. (Even as recently as 1971, a band of protesters led by Jean-Paul Sartre and filmmaker Jean-Luc Godard decided to occupy Sacré-Coeur to protest against government repression.)

Nevertheless, the expropriation was voted, and the church raised money for the project by public subscription. Donors bought one or more stones, with the price determined by the location of the stone: A hidden stone cost 120 francs (18€/$23), but a pillar stone sold for 5,000 to 100,000 francs (762€–15,245€/$953–$19,056).

Construction began in 1876, and the basilica was consecrated on October 16, 1919, which was enough time to arouse another storm of criticism. The neo-Byzantine style of architecture infuriated many Parisians, who scornfully referred to it as Notre-Dame-de-la-Galette. "A monstrous efflorescence," sniffed Emile Zola, who in one novel advocated dynamiting it. "White cheese," pronounced surrealist writer Louis Aragon.

Like many monuments that were initially unpopular (the Tour Eiffel comes to mind), Sacré-Coeur has gradually insinuated itself into the landscape of the city and is now one of the most visited monuments in Paris. The gleaming white stone was chosen for its ability to secrete calcium when it rains, making it a self-whitening church (and also, possibly, a self-dissolving church). The dome rises 78m (256 ft.) and contains one of the world's heaviest bells, weighing in at 19 tons. Notice the two equestrian statues outside; one is of St. Louis, the other of Joan of Arc.

Sadly, most of the stained-glass windows were shattered during a World War II air attack on Gare de la Chapelle, but you'll find some wonderful mosaics around the church, including Luc Olivier Meron's *Great Mosaic of Christ* (1912–22). In the ambulatory are two Renaissance-style silver statues of the Virgin Mary by P. Brunet. You can tour the dome with a guard stationed on the first terrace and enjoy spectacular views over Paris.

When you come out of the church, go down the flight of stairs that leads to the funicular and follow the road right. Immediately after the funicular, go down the stairs on the left, called rue Chappe, and you'll arrive at:

26. **Rue Gabrielle.** After the hurly-burly upstairs, you'll find this street surprisingly calm and residential. Turn right. **No. 49** was Pablo Picasso's first studio in Paris in 1900. He came here for the World Exhibition because one of his paintings had been selected for the Spanish section. He enjoyed himself in Montmartre, frequenting the Moulin Rouge and the Moulin de la Galette. Montmartre's nightlife inspired two of his paintings, *Le Moulin de la Galette* and *Le Cancan*.

Follow rue Gabrielle as it turns into rue Ravignan, which leads you to the cobblestoned:

27. **Place Emile-Goudeau.** At **no. 13** on your right is the **Bateau-Lavoir,** a small building that many artists have called home, including Picasso from 1904 to 1912. Here he painted his portrait of Gertrude Stein, *The Third Rose,* as well as *Les Demoiselles d'Avignon*. Other residents included Juan Gris from 1906 to 1922; Modigliani in 1908; Max Jacob in 1911; and Charpentier in 1912. Look at the photographs, including one of a very young Picasso. The original building burned in 1970 but was rebuilt in 1978; the studios now house 25 artists and sculptors.

In the center of the square is a **Wallace fountain,** one of 66 in Paris that were donated in 1871 by English philanthropist Richard Wallace. Intended to ameliorate the chronic water shortage in Paris, these graceful bronze fountains were created by Charles Lebourg.

The stairs at the end of the square take you to rue Ravignan. Follow it down to rue des Abbesses, turn left, and you'll be back at the Abbesses Métro station. Part II begins where you are now.

PART II   THE BOULEVARDS

Start: Place des Abbesses (Métro: Abbesses).

Finish: Cimetière de Montmartre.

Time: About 2 hours, depending on how much time you spend in the cemetery.

Best Time: Any time during the day.

Worst Time: At night, when the boulevards clog up with tour buses.

This part of the walk takes you through boulevards de Rochechouart and de Clichy, which lie just outside the former wall of the infamous *fermiers généraux* (farmer generals). These hated walls were built in 1784 so that a group of financiers could control the distribution of goods in Paris. The walls, and the system that encouraged them, were among the first targets of revolutionary rage.

On the other hand, without the walls this neighborhood might never have attracted the cabarets and dance halls that became indelibly linked with Belle Epoque Paris. Within the walls, the *fermiers généraux* levied a high tax on wine, but just outside them people were free to drink cheap local wine that was produced in abundance in the countryside. Establishments offering wine and entertainment were especially plentiful here, as Montmartre and neighboring villages had a tradition of winemaking that had begun with the Mother Superior of the Montmartre abbey.

The cabaret tradition was well installed by the time that Toulouse-Lautrec arrived on the scene to immortalize the can-can dancers at the Moulin Rouge. The "red windmill" is the last survivor of the 19th-century pleasure palaces that once lined these boulevards. Nightlife is still going strong here, even if it has taken on a rather seedy tone. As you pass the string of peep shows and sex shops on the way to the Moulin Rouge, you might find it amusing to remember that the cancan was once thought shocking. *Note:* Parts of boulevard de Clichy may not be appropriate for children. The depictions of the local talent are graphic.

● ● ● ● ● ● ● ● ● ● ● ● ● ● ●

Begin your walk at:

1. **Place des Abbesses** and take rue des Abbesses downhill on the south side of the square. You'll cross rue des Martyrs and then continue on rue d'Orsel to place Charles-Dullin, where you'll find the:

2. **Théâtre de l'Atelier,** set up in 1921 by Charles Dullin (1885–1949) in the old Théâtre de Montmartre. Dullin was an actor/director/producer who was famous for his experimental dramas and introduced the works of Pirandello to French audiences. Other playwrights whose work has appeared and continues to appear here are Jean Anouilh, Chekhov, Harold Pinter, and Samuel Beckett.

    Take rue Dancourt downhill and make a right onto:

3. **Boulevard de Rochechouart,** the main artery of northern Paris that's clogged with cars, city buses, and tour buses. It was named after Marguerite de Rochechouart, abbess of Montmartre from 1717 to 1727. The striking 1930s-style building with portholes at **no. 120** is **La Cigale,** a popular venue for jazz, pop, and rock concerts that opened in 1887. Music-hall stars Mistinguette and Maurice Chevalier regularly performed here, and in 1924, Jean Cocteau presented an adaptation of Shakespeare's *Romeo et Juliette* in which he played Mercutio. The interior was redecorated by designer Philippe Starck in 1987.

    Boulevard de Rochechouart becomes boulevard de Clichy at:

4. **Rue des Martyrs,** which comes to life when the sun goes down. At **no. 75** is the **Divan du Monde,** a 300-seat hall presenting a wide variety of music—rock, hard rock, folk, salsa, and more esoteric styles. **Madame Arthur** at **no. 75** and **Chez Michou** at **no. 80** maintain the French

Montmartre: The Boulevards

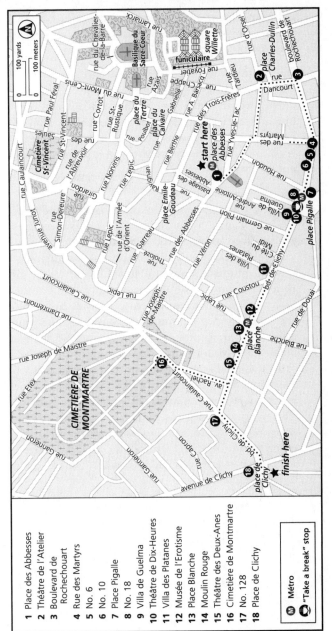

1 Place des Abbesses
2 Théâtre de l'Atelier
3 Boulevard de
   Rochechouart
4 Rue des Martyrs
5 No. 6
6 No. 10
7 Place Pigalle
8 No. 18
9 Villa de Guelma
10 Théâtre de Dix-Heures
11 Villa des Platanes
12 Musée de l'Erotisme
13 Place Blanche
14 Moulin Rouge
15 Théâtre des Deux-Anes
16 Cimetière de Montmartre
17 No. 128
18 Place de Clichy

Ⓜ Métro
Ⓒ "Take a break" stop

cabaret tradition, while other tastes are satisfied by the transvestite prostitutes who ply their trade on the street.

Continue on boulevard de Clichy to:

5. **No. 6.** In 1912, Edgar Degas moved to an apartment here after his former apartment was scheduled for demolition. "I'm not working anymore since I've moved," complained the 78-year-old painter in a letter. "It's funny, I haven't put anything away, everything is there, against the walls. I don't care, I leave everything. Age is amazing, how one becomes indifferent."

Continue along to:

6. **No. 10,** where composer Darius Milhaud (1892–1974) lived for almost 50 years. He began his studies at the Paris Conservatory but later incorporated jazz, polytonality, and Brazilian elements into his music. His first major success was providing music for Jean Cocteau's ballet *Le Boeuf sur le toit (The Nothing-Doing Bar)* in 1920. Milhaud, Arthur Honegger, Francis Poulenc, Erik Satie, and other composers formed a group called "les six," which reacted against the Impressionism of Claude Debussy and Maurice Ravel.

In 1940, Milhaud became a professor of music at the all-women Mills College in California. Ultimately he became a professor of composition at Paris's National Conservatory. Among his most famous operas are *Le Pauvre Matelot* (1926) and *Christophe Colomb* (1928), featuring a libretto by Paul Claudel, the poet and essayist, and brother of sculptor Camille Claudel.

Straight ahead is:

7. **Place Pigalle,** built by painter Jean-Baptiste Pigalle in the 19th century on the site of a gate in the *fermiers généraux* wall. Before it became the "pig alley" of World War II fame, the square was popular with 19th-century artists and writers. **No. 9** was an artists' cafe, La Nouvelle Athènes, frequented by Manet, Degas, Renoir, and Pissarro. Degas's painting *L'Absinthe,* now in the Musée d'Orsay (see Walking Tour 4, Stop 16), was set in the cafe. **No. 11,** a former artists' studio, was once the **Folies Pigalle** (a flamboyant disco) and has recently returned into seedy operation.

Before she gained fame, the "little sparrow," Edith Piaf, used to sing in the alleys off place Pigalle, hoping to earn enough money for a hot meal.

Continue along boulevard de Clichy. James Whistler had a studio at:

8. **No. 18,** where he painted *Symphony in White No. 1,* a controversial work that was refused by the Royal Academy of London and the Salon of 1863 in Paris. Finally accepted by the Salon des Refusés (Salon of the Refused), the painting was strongly criticized for its radical realism.

☕ **Take a Break** Formerly called Le Pigalle, the cafe **Le Chào-bà** is at **no. 22.** The 1950s-style decoration was radically reformed in 1995 by Hubert de Givenchy, nephew of the fashion designer. The comfortable wicker furnishings lend a neocolonial air to the spacious place, and Vietnamese flavors liven up the traditional cafe cuisine.

Continuing on boulevard de Clichy, you'll come to the cul-de-sac:

9. **Villa de Guelma** between **nos. 28** and **30.** The building at **no. 5** contains studios that were rented by Georges Braque (1882–1963); Suzanne Valadon with her son, Utrillo; and the Fauvist Raoul Dufy (1877–1953), who lived here from 1911 until his death. In his painting *30 ans ou la vie en rose,* he depicted the dining room of his apartment decorated with printed fabrics that he designed.

Return to boulevard de Clichy and proceed to **no. 36,** the:

10. **Théâtre de Dix-Heures,** which specializes in satire. Before it was turned into a cabaret, La Lune Rousse, in 1904, it was the residence of Honoré Daumier (1808–79). The artist, who had always had precarious finances, lived here from 1863 to 1869. His fortunes improved when he was hired to do a series of lithographs on the themes of clowns and Don Quixote for a local magazine.

Further on at **no. 60,** notice the:

11. **Villa les Platanes.** Built in 1895, this intriguing neo-Renaissance complex is closed to the public. However, you can look through the iron gate for a view of the splendid

vaulted ceilings that form an entrance hall and the ornate main building at the end of a long courtyard.

The building at **no. 62** had an Italian-style cafe, Le Tambourin, where van Gogh, Emile Bernard, and Toulouse-Lautrec showed their work in 1885. The cafe closed after running afoul of the police but reopened in the 1920s as Le Cyrano, a favorite cafe of the surrealists.

At **no. 72** you'll come to the:

12. **Musée de l'Erotisme (Museum of Erotic Art),** a surprisingly tasteful collection of sculpture, drawings, figurines, ornaments, and jewelry on the theme of eroticism. The first three floors display traditional erotic art from around the world—Japanese porcelain, Yoruba masks from Nigeria, delicate Chinese prints, Indian temple ornaments, and pre-Columbian fertility idols. The top two floors are devoted to rotating exhibits of contemporary erotic art. Though some pieces undoubtedly skirt the edges of vulgarity, the wit and imagination that artists throughout the ages have brought to the subject of human sexuality make a fascinating visit. The museum also has a shop where you can buy unusual key rings and other objects. Open daily from 10am to 2am, the museum has the longest visiting hours in Paris. There's an admission fee.

Continue along boulevard de Clichy and you'll arrive at:

13. **Place Blanche,** named for the white *(blanche)* plaster dust from the Montmartre quarries. The plaster arrived from rue Lepic and entered Paris through the gate in the *fermiers généraux* wall. Directly after place Blanche you'll come to the:

14. **Moulin Rouge,** which opened October 6, 1889, as a combination dance hall and amusement park. Monkeys roamed an immense garden, an orchestra played, and people drank and danced. At the center of the garden was a huge wooden elephant whose stomach contained a belly-dancing show—open to men only. In 1891, Toulouse-Lautrec painted *La Goulue* (the stage name of Louise Weber), which was the first of many portraits he executed of Moulin Rouge dancers. La Goulue's performances were legendary. In 1890, the Prince of Wales, the

Toulouse-Lautrec's Women

Jane Avril (1868–1943). Born to an Italian emigrant and a French mother, Jane Avril performed at the Moulin Rouge at age 20 and was called "the dance incarnate" by her admirers. She died in relative obscurity, even though Toulouse-Lautrec immortalized her in several posters.

Marie-Louise Fuller (1862–1928). Hailing from Illinois, Marie-Louise Fuller abandoned vaudeville and opera to become a dancer, making her Paris debut at the Folies-Bergère. Fuller was known for her performances on a glass platform floodlit from beneath. The mirrors she had set up behind and around her reflected only a silhouette, so, as one critic wrote, she looked like a "genie who dances." During her time in Paris, it is said, she had an affair with Rodin.

Yvette Guilbert (1867–1944). Appearing at the Moulin Rouge, she became famous for her silhouette of green satin and her long black gloves. Toulouse-Lautrec enjoyed painting her, and when she wasn't available but her gloves were, he painted just her gloves.

future Edward VII, reserved a front-row table to watch her perform the cancan. Recognizing him, La Goulue, leg in the air and head in her skirts, called out, "Hey, Wales, the champagne's on you!"

In 1902, the garden was transformed into a cabaret theater that quickly became the hottest show in Paris. People came for the cancan and the "chahut," a high-kicking dance that was a forerunner of the numbers performed by the Rockettes today in New York City's Radio City Music Hall.

The performer most closely identified with the Moulin Rouge was Mistinguette (1874–1956), who performed there regularly from 1907 to 1939. She was born in humble circumstances as Jeanne Bourgeois and became enormously popular as a singer and dancer. Here's what Janet Flanner wrote about her on her death:

She started her career in 1890, and for forty-nine years her Parisian genius was her figure, her optimistic brio, her penetrating, touching voice, her thirty-two white indestructible teeth (she had them all till the end), and her million-dollar legs (always prudently covered with wool fleshings, against drafts, beneath her silk tights).

In 1911, she met Maurice Chevalier, and they became a formidable entertainment team.

Other performers who've appeared at the Moulin Rouge are Edith Piaf with her protégé, Yves Montand; Charles Aznavour; Lena Horne; Bing Crosby; Ginger Rogers; Liza Minnelli; and Frank Sinatra. Today, the Moulin Rouge's show still features world-famous bare-breasted cancan dancers, provocatively draped with ostrich feathers and covered in rhinestones—but rare is the Parisian who'd be caught dead there. The glitzy, expensive show continues to pack in tourists by the busload, even more so since the film *Moulin Rouge* was released in 2001 to critical acclaim and great box-office success.

Continue along boulevard de Clichy. **No. 90** is a popular three-story disco, **La Locomotive,** and at **no. 100,** notice the:

15. **Théâtre des Deux-Anes,** which has survived in various forms since 1910. When it was called the Cabaret des Truands from 1914 to 1918, dadaist director Tristan Rémy used to serve fried potatoes during the productions. The facade is amusing, decorated with two donkeys *(ânes)* in evening clothes.

No. 104 was the studio of painter/teacher Fernand Cormon (1845–1924), whose students included van Gogh and Toulouse-Lautrec. Then take a stroll up the **cité Veron** at **no. 94.** This narrow alley overhung with trees and plants is an oasis of quiet off the bawdy boulevard.

Continue along boulevard de Clichy and turn right on avenue Rachel, at the end of which is the entrance to the:

16. **Cimetière de Montmartre,** founded in 1798 on the site of gypsum quarries. As you enter, stop at the main office to pick up a map—it's not great, but it does give a

general idea of where to find other graves not covered below.

Begin by going around the circle to the left and up the stairs, where you'll find the grave of **Emile Zola** (1840–1902), the French novelist who earned his income as a journalist. As a novelist, he took a scientific approach to his writing, describing everything in minute detail. At one time he was so poor that he had to sell his raincoat and pants and stay home working in only his shirt. His remains have since been moved to the Panthéon.

Continue around the circle and make a right on avenue Dubuisson, taking it to avenue Berlioz. Turn left on avenue Berlioz and approach the grave of the French composer **Louis-Hector Berlioz** (1803–69), just beyond chemin Artot on the left side of the street. Berlioz started out in medicine but gave that up to go to the Paris Conservatory. Composed in a loose form, his music has a highly emotional style. He won the Prix de Rome in 1830 and over the next decade composed *Romeo et Juliette.*

Cross avenue Berlioz and go left on avenue Cordier. On the left you'll see the simple black-marble stone of French new wave filmmaker **François Truffaut** (1932–84), whose works include *The 400 Blows* (1959) and *Jules and Jim* (1961). Continue on avenue Cordier to the grave of French painter **Jean-Honoré Fragonard** (1732–1806) on the left. (If you get to the next intersection, you've gone too far. It's located fairly close to the intersection of av. Berlioz and av. Cordier, about four rows back. You might have to ask for help in finding this plain gravestone.) Fragonard won the Prix de Rome and studied in Italy from 1756 to 1761. Much of his painting consists of scenes of erotic love, though after he married his works lost their sensual quality.

Continue along avenue Cordier to the grave of **Théophile Gautier,** on the right. Gautier (1811–72), a poet/novelist who sidelined as a critic, was a member of the group that believed in "art for art's sake." In his writing he adhered to a theory of "plasticity," by which he meant that a writer should create art by manipulating words in the same way a painter manipulates paint or a sculptor manipulates whatever medium he or she uses.

His best-known works are *Le Capitaine Fracasse* (1863) and *Emaux et camées* (1852).

Proceed to avenue du Montebello. Turn right and ascend a flight of stairs to the grave of Impressionist painter **Hilaire Germain Edgar Degas** (1834–1917). He's buried in his family tomb; as you'll see, the original family name was de Gas. Degas was first a student of law, then a student of Ingres; his artistic career began at the Ecole des Beaux-Arts. Later, he broke from traditional style and joined the Impressionists. His favorite subjects were ballet dancers and women at their toilette. As his eyesight failed and made painting in oils difficult (because of the detail required), he began using pastels and charcoal. Degas had a profound influence on Toulouse-Lautrec and Picasso and aided in Mary Cassatt's career.

Once Degas was present at an auction where one of his paintings was being sold for an astonishing amount. Someone asked him how he felt (supposing that he'd think it a great honor). He replied, "I feel as a horse must feel when the beautiful cup is given to the jockey."

Descend the stairs and go around to avenue du Tunnel. Turn right on avenue des Carrières. When you get to avenue des Anglais, go left to the grave of composer **Léo Delibes** (1836–91). Delibes attended the Paris Conservatory. Once an accompanist at the Paris Opéra, he went on to enjoy success with the ballets *Coppélia* (1870) and *Sylvia* (1876) and the opera *Lakmé* (1883), from which the Flower Duet is the most famous.

Continue down avenue des Anglais to the grave of **Jacques Offenbach** (Jacob Eberst, 1819–80). A darling of the Second Empire, he was conductor at the Théâtre Française in 1849 and particularly successful as a composer of operettas. During his lifetime he composed over a hundred of them, including *La Vie parisienne* (1866) and *Tales of Hoffman* (found after his death in 1880). Offenbach spent every waking moment with his music.

Continue down avenue des Anglais to avenue Samson, then turn left and cross avenue du Tunnel. On your left is the grave of **Vaslav Nijinsky** (1890–1950), the amazing Russian-born ballet dancer/choreographer. His brilliant career with Sergei Diaghilev's Ballets Russes in Paris included starring roles in *Le Spectre de la Rose, Petroushka, Prelude to the Afternoon of a Faun,* and *Le Sacre du Printemps.* After the end of his affair with Diaghilev, Nijinsky married Romola Pulski, but their marriage was fraught with trouble as Nijinsky fought to prove himself as a choreographer. Sadly, he succumbed to mental illness in 1919 and never danced again.

Continue to avenue Montmorency and turn right. Then make a left at avenue de la Croix, where you'll see the grave of **Stendhal** (Marie-Henri Beyle, 1783–1842) on the right. As a dragoon in Napoléon's army, he traveled to Italy; it was in Milan in 1814 that he launched his literary career by writing one of his two great novels: *Le Rouge et le noir* (*The Red and the Black,* 1831). Stendhal wrote the other, *The Charterhouse of Parma* (1839), while traveling around France during a leave of absence from his work as a consul.

Follow avenue de la Croix (onto which you walked when you crossed av. de Montmorency) straight out to the circle at the cemetery entrance. Go right around the circle, back to avenue Rachel. Follow this avenue out of the cemetery and walk to boulevard de Clichy, where you turn right. Cross the wide rue Caulaincourt and turn left. You are still on boulevard de Clichy. Continue to:

17. **No. 128,** once the Café Hippodrome, scene of a sad drama that had a profound effect on Picasso. Painter Charles Casagemas (1881–1901)—a close friend of Picasso's at the beginning of the 20th century—became smitten with a model named Germaine. The affair developed problems, however, and Casagemas decided to return to Barcelona. The evening before his departure, he gathered his friends at the Hippodrome, pulled a gun, and tried to kill Germaine before turning the gun on himself. Picasso devoted several canvases to Casagemas, but they remained private until 1965. "It was in thinking about the death of Casagemas that I began to paint in blue," he later wrote a friend.

Painter Georges Seurat (1859–91) took an apartment on the fifth floor at **no. 128 bis,** where he lived from 1884 to 1889. With Paul Signac, Pissarro, and others, he founded the Society of Independent Artists, which tried to find ways for artists to present their works directly to the public without first going through a panel of judges. Paul Signac was Seurat's neighbor at **no. 130,** and his studio hosted Monday-night get-togethers for the neo-Impressionists in the neighborhood. Boulevard de Clichy after a snowfall was the inspiration for one of Signac's most famous paintings: *Paris, boulevard de Clichy.*

At the foot of the hill is:

18. **Place de Clichy,** which had been another gate in the *fermiers généraux* wall. The gate was the scene of a heroic last stand by General Moncey in 1814 as the Russians and British closed in on Paris. In 1863, the town council erected the dramatic statue in the center of the square in Moncey's honor. The pedestal contains a battlefield scene in bas-relief recalling the defense of Paris and is topped by General Moncey protecting a woman who represents Paris.

You are now at the Clichy Métro station, the ending point of this walk.

The Père-Lachaise Cemetery

Start: Boulevard de Ménilmontant and avenue Principale (Métro: Père-Lachaise).

Finish: Boulevard de Ménilmontant and avenue Principale.

Time: 2 to 3 hours, depending on how many detours you take.

Best Time: Any time during the day.

Worst Time: There's no worst time to visit the cemetery, except perhaps in a driving rainstorm.

Brooding and melancholy, Père-Lachaise may be the world's most romantic cemetery. Trees teeming with black crows droop over elaborately carved mausoleums while stray cats roam through the foliage and around the tombs. Scarcely a sound disturbs the otherworldly calm of the 43-hectare (107-acre) graveyard.

The Père-Lachaise Cemetery

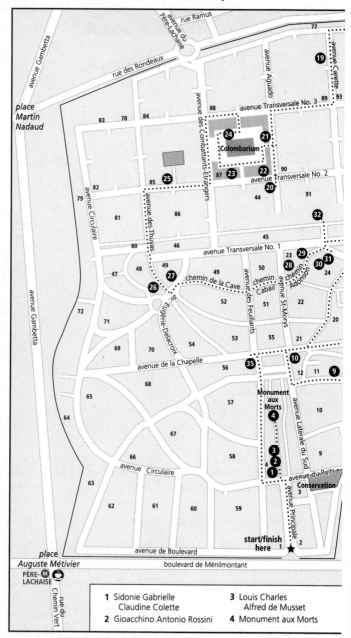

1 Sidonie Gabrielle Claudine Colette
2 Gioacchino Antonio Rossini
3 Louis Charles Alfred de Musset
4 Monument aux Morts

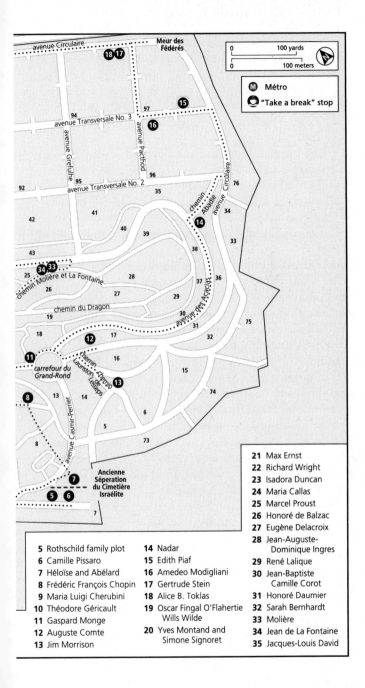

avenue Circulaire

Meur des
Fédérés

18 **17**

0 ____ 100 yards
0 ____ 100 meters

Ⓜ Métro
☕ "Take a break" stop

94
avenue Transversale No. 3

97

15

avenue Pachod

16

avenue Greffulhe

92

95
avenue Transversale No. 2

96

35

76

chemin Abadie

avenue Circulaire

34

14

42

41

40

39

38

33

43

34 **33**

25

chemin Molière et La Fontaine

26

28

27

29

37

36

chemin du Dragon

19

30

31

75

18

12

17

16

32

11

carrefour du
Grand-Rond

chemin
Lauriston

chemin
Lesseps

13

15

avenue des Acacias

8

13

14

74

avenue Casimir-Perrier

6

5

73

7

Ancienne
Séperation
du Cimetière
Israélite

5 **6**

7

5 Rothschild family plot	**14** Nadar	**21** Max Ernst
6 Camille Pissaro	**15** Edith Piaf	**22** Richard Wright
7 Héloïse and Abélard	**16** Amedeo Modigliani	**23** Isadora Duncan
8 Frédéric François Chopin	**17** Gertrude Stein	**24** Maria Callas
9 Maria Luigi Cherubini	**18** Alice B. Toklas	**25** Marcel Proust
10 Théodore Géricault	**19** Oscar Fingal O'Flahertie Wills Wilde	**26** Honoré de Balzac
11 Gaspard Monge		**27** Eugène Delacroix
12 Auguste Comte	**20** Yves Montand and Simone Signoret	**28** Jean-Auguste-Dominique Ingres
13 Jim Morrison		**29** René Lalique
		30 Jean-Baptiste Camille Corot
		31 Honoré Daumier
		32 Sarah Bernhardt
		33 Molière
		34 Jean de La Fontaine
		35 Jacques-Louis David

It's no wonder that Père-Lachaise has become the final resting place for Paris's most prestigious names: Molière, La Fontaine, Beaumarchais, Delacroix, Ingres, Balzac, Chopin, Corot, Bizet, Musset, Comte, Wilde, Bernhardt, Proust, Modigliani, Apollinaire, Duncan, Colette, Stein and Toklas, Piaf, Callas, Morrison, and Signoret and Montand, to name but a few.

Père-Lachaise's reputation as a graveyard of the great was deliberately planned by its developer, Nicolas Frochot. The land that was originally the country retreat of Père François de la Chaise d'Aix, confessor to Louis XIV, became the property of the city in 1803. As Prefect of Paris, M. Frochot was given the responsibility of turning the overgrown terrain into a cemetery. The architect in charge, Alexandre Brongniart, wanted to make a new kind of cemetery that would resemble a lush garden filled with statuary; to sell the public on this novel idea, Frochot decided to promote it as a cemetery for celebrities. His first acquisitions were the remains of Molière and La Fontaine, which aroused some interest, but when the remains of famous lovers Abélard and Héloïse were transferred here in 1817, the cemetery's popularity was assured.

In designing several tombs himself, Brongniart encouraged the families that bought plots to turn Père-Lachaise into a showcase for funereal art. Throughout the 19th century, the best architects and sculptors were hired to adorn the plots with fine stonework, and the tombs acquired a remarkable originality. The streets and lanes of this "city of the dead" contain works by Viollet-le-Duc, Charles Garnier (designer of the Paris Opéra), Hector Guimard (designer of the Art Nouveau Métro stations; see Walking Tour 6, Part I, Stop 1), Louis-Joachim Visconti, and David d'Angers.

Initially, neoclassicism was fashionable, and designers drew inspiration from Greek, Roman, or Egyptian models. Pyramids, stelae, obelisks, and columns characterize the period, as well as ornamentation borrowed from antiquity, such as urns, amphorae, and laurel crowns. Viollet-le-Duc popularized neo-Gothic designs like bats, roses, weeping women, and demons. Flowery epitaphs were often engraved on the tombs, evoking the deceased's life and accomplishments.

After 1830, the popular taste turned to the construction of ostentatious chapels that usually sheltered several graves beneath an altar and prayer bench. Their ease of access gave rise to the persistent rumor that black-magic rituals were conducted there at night. As the chapels spread throughout the area in the last half of the 19th century, the amount of garden space slowly diminished.

The cemetery's oldest part lies after the main entrance and has been listed as a National Monument. On this part of the walk you'll find the most evocative statuary-filled lanes. As you cross the avenue Transversale No. 1, you'll enter the newer portion, with straight roads and more modern tombs. The fashion for individually crafted tombs died out in the 20th century as sculpted marble was abandoned in favor of prefabricated slabs of granite.

In this walk, you can pay respects to many luminaries, but there are a few I had to leave out because of where they're located. Using a map available at the cemetery entrance, you might find others; even if you don't have a particular tomb in mind, a contemplative stroll through the cemetery's profusion of flowers and sculpture offers a glimpse of the calm eternal amid the hubbub of daily life.

● ● ● ● ● ● ● ● ● ● ● ● ● ● ● ●

Go straight up avenue Principale to the sign that says CHAPELLE. Turn left onto avenue Circulaire. The third stone on the right, black with gold lettering, marks the grave of:

1. **Sidonie Gabrielle Claudine Colette** (1873–1954). Known simply as Colette, this writer was the first woman president of the Académie Goncourt and the second woman to be made a Grand Officer of the Légion d'Honneur. Most of her writing is for and about women, the best of which are *Gigi* (1945), *The Cat* (1933), and *Chéri* (1920). Colette attributed her success as a writer (and her powers of observation) to her mother, Sidonie, whose oft-repeated advice to "Look, look!" taught her daughter to watch for life's wonders. On her deathbed in 1954, during Paris's worst thunderstorm in almost three-quarters of a century, Colette pointed at the lightning-streaked sky and said, "Look, look!" for the very last time.

Go back to avenue Principale, turn left, and walk to the grave of Italian operatic composer:

2. **Gioacchino Antonio Rossini** (1792–1868), on the left side of the path just before the sixth tree (counting from the intersection of av. Circulaire and av. Principale). During his lifetime, his operas were big box-office draws because, like *The Barber of Seville,* they featured the common person. He was indeed a commoner, but his many popular operas made him a prosperous man. When he was elderly, a group of students tried to raise money to have a statue dedicated to him. He told them, "Give me the twenty thousand and I'll stand on the pedestal myself." His remains have since been transferred to Italy.

Just beyond the next tree, also on the left, is the grave of French Romantic playwright/fiction writer/poet:

3. **Louis Charles Alfred de Musset** (1810–57), who had a long affair with George Sand that she commemorated in her 1859 book *She and He.* Underneath his bust is an inscription from one of Musset's poems that translates as:

> *My dear friends, when I die*
> *Plant a willow at the cemetery*
> *I love its weeping leaves*
> *The pallor is sweet and precious*
> *And its shadow will lighten*
> *The earth where I shall sleep.*

In front of you is the colossal:

4. **Monument aux Morts,** designed by the sculptor Bartholomé. The facade's nude figures were considered scandalous in the 19th century—in fact, on the day of the monument's inauguration, they were discreetly covered. Inside, underground chambers contain bones from abandoned mausoleums. When a mausoleum falls into disrepair and is no longer visited, the concessionaires are notified; if repairs aren't made, the neglected mausoleum's bones are exhumed, placed in labeled boxes, and deposited behind the locked doors of this monument. Curiously, those doors are outfitted with heavy brass knockers. You might try banging on them to see if anyone answers.

Go back in the direction from which you came and turn left on avenue du Puits. Take your second right, then your first left (a dirt pathway), which is avenue Rachel.

Just after the eighth tree in the front row of the cemetery's old Jewish section is the:

5. **Rothschild family plot.** A German-Jewish family whose history began with Mayer Anselm (1743–1812), the Rothschilds were one of Europe's great financial powers. Mayer Anselm, a Frankfurt moneylender, lent large sums to various governments and princes. His five sons expanded the business to Vienna, London, Naples, and Paris. The youngest, Jacob (1792–1868), started the Paris branch, and his capital was used to build the French railroad. But the most successful branch of the business was opened by Sir Nathan Mayer, who not only lent money to Wellington and the British government during wars with Napoléon, but also was the first Jewish man to be admitted to England's House of Lords.

Continue five trees down from the Rothschild plot; when you get to the second row, head to the grave site of painter/graphic artist:

6. **Camille Pissaro** (1830–1903). Born in the West Indies to a Jewish father and a creole mother, he moved to Paris in 1855. Four years later, he met Monet and became a member of the Impressionist group. Of the Impressionists, Pissaro was the oldest (by about 10 years), and though he isn't the best known of the group, he was the only one who exhibited in all eight Impressionist exhibitions.

Return to avenue du Puits and go right to the fifth tree from the corner. You'll see a Gothic structure with a fence around it. This is the grave of:

7. **Héloïse and Abélard.** In the 19th century, these tombs were a magnet for disappointed lovers. "Go when you will, you find somebody snuffling over that tomb," wrote Mark Twain in *The Innocents Abroad.*

Pierre Abélard was born near Nantes and attended the school of Notre-Dame, where he had a falling-out with his master and was expelled. Abélard then crossed the river to the Ste-Geneviève school, where he eventually became a master. By the time he was 36, he was recognized as a great scholar and, ironically, became canon and master of Notre-Dame in 1115. His presence attracted to Notre-Dame students from all over medieval Europe.

Later, while Abélard was working as the assistant to Canon Fulbert, Héloïse's uncle, he and Héloïse fell in love and were secretly married. When they were discovered, Héloïse's uncle sent her to the Argenteuil convent and had Abélard castrated; Abélard went to a monastery and not long after opened a theology school in which he challenged ecclesiastical authority. Though he remained popular with his students, his enemies charged him with heresy and persecuted him constantly.

During the time Abélard and Héloïse were separated, they always maintained their romance through letters. Abélard died in 1142, Héloïse 24 years later. Finally, after countless separations, their remains were reunited in Père-Lachaise.

Back out on avenue du Puits, turn right and proceed to chemin Mehul (an unpaved road on your left). Make a left and then take your second left (not chemin du Coq, the next one). Note that there's no name marker for this cobbled road. On the right is the grave of Polish composer:

8. **Frédéric François Chopin** (1810–49). As a child, Chopin was asked to play in the salons of Warsaw's wealthiest. When he was 21 he gave his first Paris concert, and by the time he was 29 he'd completed 24 preludes, one in each major and minor key (and none lasting more than 5 min.). He gained notoriety for introducing the piano as a solo instrument rather than an accompanying one.

About four stones down on the right is another child prodigy, Italian composer:

9. **Maria Luigi Cherubini** (1760–1842), who particularly enjoyed sacred music. By 16, he'd already written several masses and other sacred choral pieces. His work profoundly affected Beethoven's vocal works. At 60, after 4 years as a professor of composition at the Paris Conservatory, Cherubini became its director.

Turn right at avenue Laterale du Sud. Ascend two staircases and take a right on avenue de la Chapelle. On the right, just beyond the bench behind the bush, is the grave of Romantic painter:

10. **Théodore Géricault** (1791–1824). On the grave marker is a statue of Géricault with his palette, and around the

side is a bronze bas-relief of one of his paintings, *Mounted Officer of the Imperial Guard* (1812). Géricault studied in Paris with Carle Vernet and Pierre Guérin. His most famous work, *The Raft of the Medusa,* was one of the first paintings of its size to reflect a contemporary newsworthy event: the 1816 shipwreck of the *Medusa.* He was also one of the first to break traditional form in technique and is thought to have influenced Eugène Delacroix (see later in this chapter).

Return to the road and continue along to carrefour du Grand-Rond. Go left around the circle. On your left is the grave of French mathematician/physicist/public official:

11. **Gaspard Monge, comte de Péluse** (1746–1818). A friend of Napoléon, he's best known for his geometrical research and was instrumental in the 1794 founding of Paris's Ecole Polytechnique. Monge's research helped lay the foundations of modern geometry, which is essential to the mechanical drawings produced by today's architects.

Follow the road around the circle to the second left. Walk to the second tree on the left after the first possible right. On the left you'll see a black statue in the posture of a Madonna and Child. In front of that headstone is the grave of French philosopher:

12. **Auguste Comte** (1798–1857), the founder of positivism, whose goal was to create a peaceful and harmonic society. Confronting his impending death in 1857, the modest and humble Comte is reported to have said, "What an irreparable loss!"

Head back to the right turn that you passed on your way to Comte's grave: chemin Lauriston (now on your left). Make a left. When you get to the fork in the road, take the left fork (chemin de Lesseps) to the grave of the illustrious American rock singer and 1960s icon:

13. **Jim Morrison** (1943–71). This one is a little tricky to find because it's a small grave site, tucked away amid many larger tombs. The first thing you should look for is the crowd of people usually gathered here. Then look for two large trees (on the right), one of which has "God Bless America" carved into it; the other, a bit closer to the road, says "Elvis is king." Note that the headstone you see today

is a new one—the original, which was vandalized, had a marble bust of Morrison on it.

The inclusion of The Doors's lead vocalist in this prestigious cemetery is controversial: Because of the number and type of visitors Morrison's grave attracts, the surrounding area is heavily trafficked and marked with graffiti. Morrison was buried here because he fit one of the three requirements—you have to be born in Paris, die in Paris, or live in Paris. Morrison died of a drug overdose here while vacationing.

Go back the way you came to carrefour du Grand-Rond. Take your first right off the circle, which is avenue des Acacias. This is a bit of a walk, but follow this road up and around. Not far after the sign for section 38 you'll see a cement bench on your right. Just behind the cement bench is the grave of photographer:

14. **Nadar** (Gaspard Félix Tournachon, 1820–1910). Nadar was one of the greatest, if not the greatest, photographers of the 19th century. He's remembered for his stunning images of Hugo, Sand, Baudelaire, Delacroix, and Bernhardt. Eventually Nadar gave up photography and took up hot-air ballooning. It was during a balloon ride that he took the first bird's-eye-view photo of Paris.

Make your first right after Nadar's grave onto chemin Abadie. Go right on avenue Transversale No. 2 to avenue Circulaire. Turn left and walk to avenue Transversale No. 3, then turn left again. Before you get to the next grave, you should note the two **monuments to the victims of Nazi concentration camps** on your right—one from Manthausen, the other from Flossenberg.

Walk down the first dirt pathway off the right side of avenue Transversale No. 3, then take your first right (another dirt pathway) almost immediately after you get off the main road. Look for the grave of the Famille Gassion-Piaf in the second row back from the street. This is the resting place of the world-famous cabaret singer known around the world for her beautiful rendition of "La Vie En Rose":

15. **Edith Piaf** (1915–63), who was loved for her powerful, emotional voice. Dubbed the "little sparrow," she began singing in cafes and on the streets of Paris at the tender

age of 15; she was so loved by her fans that Jean Cocteau even wrote a play for her.

Return to the road and continue in the direction you were headed. Make a left on the pathway before reaching the intersection of avenue Transversale No. 3 and avenue Patchod. Just after you take the dirt pathway, go left again down to the seventh row. The second grave on the left has a very plain stone to mark the resting place of Italian painter/sculptor:

16. **Amedeo Modigliani** (1884–1920), famous for his elongated forms. Wonderfully individualistic, he became passionate about sculpture as a medium after he met Brancusi in 1909; however, the most notable influence on him was African sculpture. In spite of (probably because of) his unique style, he remained unknown until well after his death from tuberculosis—a condition aggravated by his abuse of drugs and alcohol.

Back out on avenue Transversale No. 3, turn left and go to avenue Patchod. Turn right and head to avenue Circulaire. First detour to the right to see additional **monuments to Nazi concentration-camp victims.** These immense sculptures speak much louder than any inscriptions that could be placed on the monuments themselves.

Now head back in the other direction, crossing avenue Patchod. After the fourth tree on the left is the grave of:

17. **Gertrude Stein** (1874–1946), who's perhaps best known for her line "Rose is a rose is a rose is a rose." Friends with Ernest Hemingway, Sherwood Anderson, Pablo Picasso, Sylvia Beach, and many others, Stein hosted one of the most famous weekly literary salons. She and her brother Leo were trendsetters in the art world, and she had one of the best private collections in Paris at the time.

Next to Stein's grave is what looks like an empty plot or a plot without a stone—this is the resting place of the ever-present, ever-silent:

18. **Alice B. Toklas** (1877–1966), Stein's famous-by-association lover. As always, Toklas has second billing, for she's noted on the backside of Stein's headstone. Even in death Toklas stands behind Stein—a melancholic ending for a loyal and longtime companion.

Continue along avenue Circulaire and take your second left onto avenue Carette, following it to the grave of bitingly witty writer:

19. **Oscar Fingal O'Flahertie Wills Wilde** (1854–1900). You can't miss his headstone—a massive Art Deco Egyptian-like sphinx that looks as if it might take flight. It was restored in 1992, and a sign states that it's "protected by law as an historic monument." First and foremost a dandy and an aesthete (plus a comedian), Wilde was once quoted as saying, "I put my genius into my life and my talent into my work." Some of his most famous works are *The Picture of Dorian Gray* (1891), *A Woman of No Importance* (1893), *The Importance of Being Earnest* (1895), and his fairy-tale collections. In the late 1890s, Wilde was charged with homosexual practices by the marquess of Queensbury (father of Wilde's paramour, Lord Alfred Douglas, aka Bosie) and was sentenced to 2 years' hard labor. One day, while standing handcuffed in the cold rain, he declared, "If this is the way Queen Victoria treats her prisoners, then she doesn't deserve to have any."

Continue to the next intersection and turn right on avenue Transversale No. 3. At the next intersection, go left on avenue Aguado (there's no name marker here). Cross avenue Transversale No. 2 and on your right you'll see the tomb of:

20. **Yves Montand** (1921–91) **and Simone Signoret** (1921–85), France's First Couple of film. Born in Germany to French parents, Simone Signoret was raised in Paris and moved to England with her family at the outset of World War II. She began her acting career in British films, winning the British Film Industry award for *Casque d'Or* (1952) and then an Oscar for her portrayal of Laurence Harvey's mistress in *Room at the Top* (1959). Maturing into a fine character actress, Signoret continued her film career in France until 1982.

Italian-born Yves Montand was a protégé of Edith Piaf, who featured the song-and-dance man first in her nightclub act and then in her 1946 film *Etoile sans Lumière*. Although he continued his concert appearances, Montand gained stature as a dramatic actor in Georges Clouzot's *The Wages of Fear*, Costa-Gavras's *Z*, and Claude

Berri's *Jean de Florette*. The couple married in 1951 and remained together until Signoret's death in 1985 despite Montand's many affairs, most famously with Marilyn Monroe during the filming of *Let's Make Love.* "Chains do not hold a marriage together," said Signoret in an interview. "It is threads, hundreds of tiny threads which sew people together through the years. That is what makes a marriage last—more than passion or even sex!"

Retrace your steps on avenue Aguado, crossing avenue Transversale No. 2, and turn left into the **Colombarium.** Make your first right under the covered walkway. Just before the second staircase, in the first row of the second section, fourth row from the bottom, is the marker for German-born dadaist/surrealist painter:

21. **Max Ernst** (1891–1976). Originally a psychology student at Bonn University, the man who called himself Dadamax took up painting because of his interest in the painting of psychotics. Ernst came to Paris in 1922 and joined the surrealist movement 2 years later. He lived in the United States from 1941 to 1949 and was briefly married to art patron Peggy Guggenheim; however, he returned to France in 1949 and remained until his death.

Turn around and cross the entry road you came in on to the other side (as if you had gone left rather than right on entering the Colombarium). Proceed to the end and make a right when you can't go any farther. Behind the third stair on your left is the marker of African-American writer:

22. **Richard Wright** (1908–60). Wright was born on a Mississippi plantation and joined the Federal Writers' Project in the 1930s. His many books include *Uncle Tom's Children* (1938) and *Native Son* (1940).

In December 1945, the French government invited Wright to come to Paris as its guest. He had difficulty getting a passport from the U.S. State Department. When he and his wife finally arrived in Paris by ship, they were met by the American ambassador—and none other than Gertrude Stein. Stein had, in her usual way, already managed to get in Wright's good graces by sending him a letter that read, "Dear Richard: It is obvious that you and

I are the only two geniuses of this era." Wright died at 52 in Paris and was cremated with a copy of his novel *Black Boy.*

Proceed around to the next block. Just before the first staircase, the second row up, the last stone on the right is the marker of dancer:

23. **Isadora Duncan** (Dora Gray Duncan, 1878–1927). San Francisco–born Duncan achieved fame with her flamboyant expressionism as a dancer. Wearing a scant Greek tunic and draped in a multitude of flowing scarves, she performed barefoot to music not originally written for dance. Though not received warmly in the United States, she was adored in Paris from the time of her 1922 arrival; that adoration soon spread throughout Europe. Her final performance was held in Paris.

Walk through the courtyard and around to the stairs between the two structures on the other side (those facing the one with Isadora Duncan's marker). Descend the stairs and make a right. At the end of the hallway, go left to the stone numbered 6258, on your right. This is the grave of Greek-American soprano:

24. **Maria Callas** (1923–77). Born in New York City, she moved to Greece at 13 and studied at Athens's Royal Conservatory. Callas made her debut in 1942 at the National Opera in Athens, as Tosca, which remained one of her most celebrated roles. In addition to the unusual timbre of her voice and the dramatic intensity that turned La Callas into an international sensation, she also made a serious and enduring contribution to the operatic repertoire. *Bel canto* works such as Bellini's *Norma,* Donizetti's *Lucia di Lammermoor,* and Cherubini's *Medea* were consigned to the scrap heap before Callas demonstrated how they could and should be sung. By the time she moved to Paris in 1963, her voice was crumbling, and she retired a few years later. Some say that the heartbreaking end of an affair with Aristotle Onassis (who, of course, married Jackie Kennedy) contributed to her premature death at 53.

From Callas's stone, continue straight ahead and go up the main stairs, to your right. Make a left at avenue des Combattants-Etrangers (the one directly ahead). When you get to avenue Transversale No. 2, make a right. Make another right at the first dirt pathway and walk to the fourth grave on the left, which is that of novelist:

25. **Marcel Proust** (1871–1922). The sickly son of wealthy parents, Proust is considered a truly great modern writer because of his ability to communicate the link between a person's external and internal consciousness. His writing culminated in his multivolume masterpiece, *A la recherche du temps perdu (Remembrance of Things Past),* which he began in his bed, shortly after his mother's death in 1906. Proust wanted to be buried with his friend/lover, composer Maurice Ravel, but their families wouldn't allow it.

Go back out to avenue Transversale No. 2 and turn right (in the direction you were headed before you detoured), then at the first intersection go left onto avenue des Thuyas. Continue along, crossing avenue Transversale No. 1 and then going straight. On the right, just before the next corner, is the grave of novelist:

26. **Honoré de Balzac** (1799–1850), who studied law at the Sorbonne but decided he'd rather write. He spent all day and most of the night writing, sleeping in the late afternoon for only a few hours. To support himself, he also wrote pulp novels under a pseudonym. Only a few months before his death, he married Polish countess Evelina Hanska—with whom he'd been exchanging love letters for 18 years.

Turn left at the next intersection onto avenue Eugène-Delacroix and go to the grave of painter:

27. **Eugène Delacroix** (1798–1863), one of the masters of the Romantic movement. He spent a great deal of time copying old masters at the Louvre and was an admirer of Rubens. He once announced that "if you are not skillful enough to sketch a man falling out of a window during the time it takes him to get from the fifth story to the ground, then you will never produce a monumental work." Delacroix produced many monumental works, among them *The Bark of Dante* (1922) and *The Massacre at Scios* (1824). His body of work topped more than 9,000 paintings, drawings, and pastels. He was an inspiration to many of the Impressionists, including van Gogh,

Seurat, and Renoir. Delacroix's old studio on rue de Furstemberg has been turned into a museum of his work (see Walking Tour 5, Part I, Stop 11).

Directly on your right is chemin de la Cave. Follow it, crossing avenue des Feuillants. Chemin de la Cave turns into chemin Cabail. Follow it to avenue St-Morys. Make a right on the path just past the second tree and you'll find a white stone, about three rows back, facing away from avenue St-Morys. This is the grave of painter:

28. Jean-Auguste-Dominique Ingres (1780–1867). Ingres entered David's studio (see below) at 17 and won the Prix de Rome only 4 years later. His work has a fluid, sinuous, rhythmical quality that broke with traditional classical form. In 1806, because he distorted the human figure (in his portrait of Mme Rivière) in favor of the linear rhythm of his painting, he was alienated from the Académie. That same year, in frustration, he returned to Rome, where he remained until 1820.

He returned to Paris in 1841 and lived out his life here. Two of his greatest works are *Bather of Valpincon* (1808) and *Odalisque with the Slave* (1842).

Return to avenue St-Morys and turn left. Take the first left onto chemin Adonson (the left fork) and follow it to the grave of jeweler/glassmaker:

29. René Lalique (1860–1945), the exceedingly talented Art Nouveau artisan. Most know him for his clear crystal glass engraved with frosted flowers, figures, or animals, which he began designing in 1902. However, the jewelry he made after establishing his Paris workshop in 1885 focused not on the stone but on the design. Lalique particularly enjoyed using semiprecious stones—most notably opals—bringing them back into fashion. His pieces often contained the Art Nouveau motifs of dragonflies, peacocks, and female nudes.

Continue on. The pathway veers right, and from the path you can see the tops of the heads of two sculpted busts. The black one is of landscape painter:

30. Jean-Baptiste Camille Corot (1796–1875). The son of a Paris shopkeeper, Corot worked in textile shops until around 1822 and didn't begin to study painting until he was 30. Only 5 years later he started exhibiting regularly at the Salon of the Barbizon School, a group of artists who focused primarily on landscape painting.

Corot was greatly respected by his contemporaries and influenced many younger artists, but didn't receive great acclaim until he was well into his 50s. When broke and needing to sell one of his treasured paintings, he'd exclaim in despair, "Alas, my collection has been so long complete, and now it is broken!"

Three rows behind Corot, directly in front of the big tree, is the grave of sculptor/painter/lithographer:

31. **Honoré Daumier** (1808–79). It's appropriate that Daumier is buried so near Corot, for Corot gave Daumier a house at Valmondois-sur-Seine-et-Oise when he was old, poor, nearly blind, and threatened with eviction. Most famous for his spontaneous caricature sculptures of political figures, Daumier was even imprisoned for 6 months because of his 1832 *Gargantua* cartoon showing Louis-Philippe swallowing bags of gold that had been extracted from his people.

Daumier produced approximately 100 lithographs per year in addition to his sculpture and painting. A member of the realist school, he was admired by Delacroix, Balzac, Baudelaire, and Degas. In fact, Balzac was once heard to say of Daumier, "This boy has some Michelangelo under his skin."

Return to the main path and cross avenue Transversale No. 1. To the left of the back of the big tomb in front of you is the grave of Paris-born actress:

32. **Sarah Bernhardt** (Henriette-Rosine Bernard, 1844–1923), who was raised in a convent for the first 13 years of her life. A graduate of the Paris Conservatory, she made her debut at 17 and was badly received. However, she persevered and eventually became one of Paris's best-loved actresses. Following her funeral, Janet Flanner said that "for days after what seemed like Bernhardt's last public performance, mourners stood in line in the cemetery to get a view of where she lay dead, just as they had made the box-office queue to see her alive on the stage."

She's especially well-known for her performances in Victorien Sardou's *Fédora, Théodora,* and *La Tosca;* in 1912 she even became a silent-film star.

Back on avenue Transversale No. 1, turn left and go to the dirt pathway on the right, just before the sign marking the 39th division. Make a right onto chemin Molière et La Fontaine and walk to the grave of writer/actor:

33. **Molière** (Jean-Baptiste Poquelin, 1622–73). Born in Paris, Molière was the king of French high comedy in the 17th century. His satirical plays, including *Le Tartuffe* (1664) and *Le Misanthrope* (1666), pointed out society's hypocrisies and often attacked the church. Not surprisingly, there were many problems when it came to the issue of his burial. Church officials decided that he couldn't be buried in consecrated ground, which was said to run 4m (13 ft.) deep. Louis XIV therefore ordered the grave be dug to 5m (16 ft.). Unfortunately, no one knows where the great dramatist was really buried—legend has it that he disappeared before he could be buried in that 5m- (16-ft.) deep grave, so M. Frochot (who established the cemetery) was most likely taken for a ride when he bought Molière's bones.

Right next to Molière is the grave of French poet:

34. **Jean La Fontaine** (1621–95). He and Molière are side by side, surrounded by a wrought-iron fence. La Fontaine was famous mainly for his books of fables (12 in all) featuring animals behaving like humans. The fables, modeled after Aesop's, were so successful that 137 editions were printed in his lifetime. It's probably safe to assume that if Frochot was duped in regard to Molière's bones, he was probably duped about La Fontaine's as well.

Keep going to the end, taking the left fork and following it all the way back down to avenue de la Chapelle. Turn right and pass Géricault's grave (on your left). Go left on the other side of the park and proceed to the fifth grave on the right, that of neoclassicist French painter:

35. **Jacques-Louis David** (1748–1825), known to most people as just David. His first attempt at the Prix de Rome failed and led to a suicide attempt. Fortunately, he

was saved by some fellow Académie students who found him in his room at the Louvre before it was too late.

In 1774, he did win the Prix de Rome and left to study in Italy, returning to Paris in 1780. He then became very involved in politics and even voted for the execution of Louis XVI in 1793.

David revolutionized art with his huge paintings that were allegories or commentaries on current events. From the terrace outside the Café de la Régence, he liked to sketch prisoners on their way to the guillotine—among them Marie Antoinette. Napoléon recognized David's potential as a propagandist and appointed him official painter. Between 1802 and 1805 he did a series for Napoléon, including the *Coronation of Napoléon* (1805–07, at the Louvre). When Napoléon fell, David went into exile in Brussels. His influence can be seen in the work of Ingres, Gérard, and Gros.

Continue down the steps to avenue du Puits. Make a left to avenue Principale, then make a right on avenue Principale and continue to the exit. For the Métro, go to the Père-Lachaise station at which you arrived. Or:

Take a Break   A simple but charming eatery, **Aux Tables du Père Lachaise** at **44 bd. Ménilmontant** serves excellent homemade French fare with a menu that changes daily.

Essentials

P aris may be one of Europe's largest cities, but you'll find it's a surprisingly easy metropolis to navigate. The following is an overview of the practical information that you'll need to make your visit a hassle-free success. For fuller coverage, consult *Frommer's Paris* or *Frommer's France*.

TOURIST INFORMATION

At the main **tourist office,** 127 av. des Champs-Elysées, 8e (© **08-92-68-30-00;** www.parisinfo.com; info@paris-tourist office.com), you can secure information about both Paris and the provinces. It's open daily (except May 1) 9am to 8pm. Sundays and winter holidays from November to March the hours are 11am to 7pm.

Welcome Offices in the city center will also give you free maps, brochures, and *Paris Monthly Information,* an English-language listing of current events and performances.

CITY LAYOUT

Paris is surprisingly compact. The 20 *arrondissements* (districts) of Paris occupy 104 sq. km (40 sq. miles) and contain about 1.9 million inhabitants. The **river Seine** divides Paris into **the Right Bank** *(Rive Droite)* to the north and the **Left Bank** *(Rive Gauche)* to the south. These designations make sense when you stand on a bridge and face downstream, watching the waters flow out toward the sea—to your right is the north bank, to your left the south. Thirty-two bridges link the Right Bank and the Left Bank, some providing access to the two small islands at the heart of the city: **Ile de la Cité,** the city's birthplace and site of Notre-Dame, and **Ile St-Louis,** an oasis of sober 17th-century mansions. These islands can confuse walkers who think that they've just crossed a bridge from one bank to the other, only to find themselves caught in an almost medieval maze of narrow streets and old buildings.

MAIN ARTERIES & STREETS   Between 1860 and 1870, Baron Georges-Eugène Haussmann, at the request of Napoléon III, forever changed the look of Paris by creating the legendary **boulevards:** St-Michel, St-Germain, Haussmann, Malesherbes, Sébastopol, Magenta, Voltaire, and Strasbourg.

The "main street" on the Right Bank is, of course, the **avenue des Champs-Elysées,** beginning at the Arc de Triomphe and running to place de la Concorde. Haussmann also created **avenue de l'Opéra,** plus the **12 avenues** radiating like the points of a star from the Arc de Triomphe. This design gave the square its original name: place de l'Etoile (*étoile* means "star"). Following de Gaulle's death it was renamed in his honor; today it's often referred to as place Charles-de-Gaulle–Etoile.

Haussmann also cleared the Ile de la Cité of its medieval buildings, turning it into a showcase for Notre-Dame. Finally, he laid out two parks on the western and southeastern fringes of the city: the **Bois de Boulogne** and **Bois de Vincennes.**

FINDING AN ADDRESS   The city of Paris is divided into 20 municipal wards called arrondissements, each with its own mayor, city hall, police station, and central post office. Most city maps are divided according to these arrondissements, and all addresses include the arrondissement number (written in Roman or Arabic numerals and followed by *e* or *er*). For more information, see *Frommer's Paris* or *Frommer's France.*

Numbers on buildings running parallel to the Seine most often follow the course of the river—east to west. On perpendicular streets, numbers on buildings begin low closer to the river.

MAPS   If you're staying for more than 2 or 3 days, purchase an inexpensive pocket-size book that includes the *plan de Paris* by arrondissement, available at all major newsstands and bookshops. Most of these guides provide a Métro map, a fold-out city map, and indexed arrondissement maps, with all streets listed and keyed.

GETTING AROUND

Paris is a city for strollers whose greatest joy in life involves rambling through unexpected alleyways and squares. Given a choice of conveyance, make it your own two feet whenever possible. Only when you can't walk another step or are in a hurry to reach an exact destination should you consider the following swift and prosaic means of urban transport.

BY SUBWAY   The **Métro** (© **08-92-68-77-14** for information in English; www.ratp.fr) is the most efficient and easy means of transport. The lines are numbered, and the final destination of each is clearly marked on subway maps, on the trains themselves, and in the underground passageways. Note that there's a **Métro map** on the inside back cover of this book. Most stations display a map of the system at the entrance. Figure out the route from where you are to your destination, noting the stations where you'll have to change.

To make sure you catch the correct train, find your destination, then visually follow that line out beyond your stop to the very end of its route and remember the station name: That is the all-important *direction* you will need to find in the stations and displayed on trains. Transfer stations are known as *correspondances*. (Some require long walks—Châtelet is the most notorious.)

Most trips require only one transfer. Many larger stations have maps with push-button indicators that help you plot your route more easily by lighting up automatically when you press the button for your destination. A ride on the urban lines costs the same to any point.

On the Sceaux, Noissy–St-Léger, and St-Germain-en-Laye lines serving the suburbs, fares are based on distance. A *carnet* (ticket book) of 10 tickets is the best buy. You can also purchase the *Formule 1,* allowing unlimited travel on the city's network of subways for 1 day, or the *Paris Visite,* valid for 2, 3, or 5 days.

At the station entrance, buy your ticket, then insert it into the turnstile and pass through. At some exits tickets are checked, so hold on to yours. There are occasional ticket checks on the trains, platforms, and passageways, too.

If you're changing trains, get out and determine toward which *direction* (final destination) on the next line you want to head, then follow the bright-orange CORRESPONDANCE signs until you reach the proper platform. Don't follow a SORTIE sign (Exit) or you'll have to pay another fare to resume your journey.

The Métro starts running daily at 5:30am and closes around 1am. It's reasonably safe at any hour, but beware of pickpockets.

BY BUS   Travel by bus is slower than that by subway, but it's also an excellent and comfortable way to see more of the city. Most buses run 6:30am to 9:15pm (a few operate until 12:30am; a handful operate during early morning hours). Service is limited on Sunday and holidays. Bus and Métro fares are the same, and you can use the same tickets on both.

Each bus shelter has a route map that you should check carefully. Because of the number of one-way streets, the bus is likely to make different stops depending on its direction. Destinations are usually listed north to south and east to west. Most stops along the way are also posted on the sides of the buses. To catch a bus, wait in line at the bus stop. Signal the driver to stop the bus and board in order.

If you intend to use buses frequently, pick up an RATP bus map at any Métro station.

BY TAXI   It's impossible to secure a taxi at rush hour, so don't even try. Taxi drivers are strongly organized into an effective lobby to keep their number limited to under 15,000.

Watch out for the common rip-offs. Always check the meter to make sure that you don't have your fare added onto the previous passenger's fare. Beware of cabs without meters, which often wait for tipsy patrons outside nightclubs—and always settle the tab in advance. You can hail regular cabs on the street when their signs read LIBRE. Taxis are easier to find at the many stands near Métro stations. But be warned that on weekend nights (around 1am when the Métro stops running) and when it's pouring with rain, taxi lines can be up to an hour long.

BY BICYCLE   Paris in recent years has added many miles of right-hand lanes specifically designated for cyclists, plus hundreds of bike racks scattered throughout the city. (When these aren't available, many Parisians simply chain their bikes to the nearest fence or lamppost.) Cycling is especially popular in the larger parks and gardens.

If you want to rent a bicycle, contact **Roue Libre,** 1 Passage Mondetour, 1e (*℃* **01-44-76-86-43;** www.rouelibre.fr; Métro: Châtelet or 37 bd. Bourdon; *℃* 01-44-54-19-29; Métro: Bastille).

Note you have to leave a steep deposit to rent a bike.

BY CAR Don't seriously consider driving a car in Paris—the streets are narrow, and parking is next to impossible. Besides, many visitors don't possess the nerve, skill, and ruthlessness required to navigate the complicated mixture of streets, rotaries, signs, rules, and attitudes Paris serves up to the unsuspecting driver.

RECOMMENDED READING

Numerous books exist on all aspects of French history and society—ranging from the very general, such as the section on France in the *Encyclopedia Americana,* International Edition (Grolier, 1989), which presents an excellent illustrated overview of the French people and their way of life, to the very specific, such as Judi Culbertson and Tom Randall's *Permanent Parisians: An Illustrated Guide to the Cemeteries of Paris* (Chelsea Green, 1986), which depicts the lives of famous French and expatriates who are buried in Paris.

HISTORY In addition to the encyclopedia reference above, a broad overview of French history can be found in other encyclopedias and general history books. One very good one is *History of France,* by Guillaume de Bertier de Savigny and David H. Pinkney (Forum Press, 1983), a comprehensive history with illustrations and plenty of obscure but interesting facts.

Two books that present French life and society in the 17th century are Warren Lewis's *The Splendid Century* (William Morrow, 1978) and Madame de Sévigné's *Selected Letters,* edited by Leonard W. Tancock (Penguin, 1982), which contains imaginative and witty letters written to her daughter during the reign of Louis XIV.

Moving into the 20th century, *Pleasure of the Belle Epoque: Entertainment and Festivity in Turn-of-the-Century France,* by Charles Rearick (Yale University Press, 1985), depicts public diversions in the changing and troubled times of the Third Republic. *Paris Was Yesterday, 1925–1939* (Harcourt Brace Jovanovich, 1988) is a fascinating collection of excerpts from Janet Flanner's "Letters from Paris" column of the *New Yorker.* Larry Collins and Dominique Lapierre have written a popular history of the liberation of Paris in 1944 called *Is Paris Burning?* (Warner Books, 1991).

Finally, two unusual approaches to French history are Rudolph Chleminski's *The French at Table* (William Morrow, 1985), a funny and honest history of why the French know how to eat better than anyone and how they go about it, and *Paris: A Century of Change, 1878-1978,* by Normal Evenson (Yale University Press, 1979), a notable study of the urban development of Paris.

TRAVEL   Since 1323 some 10,000 books have been devoted to exploring Paris. One of the latest is *Paris: Capital of the World,* by Patrice Higonnet (Harvard University, 2002). This book takes a fresh social, cultural, and political look at this City of Lights. Higonnet even explores Paris as "the capital of sex," and in contrast the "capital of art." The gang's all here from Balzac to Zola.

Showing a greater fondness for gossip is Alistair Horne in his *Seven Pages of Paris* (Alfred A. Knopf, 2002). From the Roman founding up to the student riots of 1968, this is one of the most amusing books on Paris we've ever read. Horne is not a timid writer. He calls the Palais de Chaillot fascistic and hideous, the Pompidou Center a horror. We even learn that a woman once jumped off the Eiffel tower, bounced off the roof of a parked car, and survived. In *The Flâneur, A Stroll Through the Paradoxes of Paris* (Bloomsbury, 2001), Edmund White wants the reader to experience Paris as Parisians do. Hard to translate exactly, *a flâneur* is someone who strolls, loafs, or idles. With White, you can circumnavigate Paris as whim dictates.

BIOGRAPHY   You can get a more intimate look at history through biographies of historical figures. The best book yet on the architect who changed the face of Paris is *Haussmann: His*

Life and Times and the Making of Modern Paris, by Patrick Camiller (Ivan R. Dee, 2002).

A Moveable Feast (Collier Books, 1987), Ernest Hemingway's recollections of Paris during the 1920s, and Morley Callaghan's *That Summer in Paris: Memories of Tangled Friendships with Hemingway, Fitzgerald and Some Others* (1963), an anecdotal account of the same period, represent the early part of the last century. Another interesting read is *The Autobiography of Alice B. Toklas,* by Gertrude Stein (Vintage Books, 1990). It's not only the account of 30 years in Paris, but also the autobiography of Gertrude Stein.

Simone de Beauvoir, by Deirdre Bair (Summit Books, 1990), was described by one critic as "a biography *à l'Americaine*'—that is to say, long, with all the warts of its subject unsparingly described." The story of the great feminist intellectual was based in part on tape-recorded conversations and unpublished letters.

Colette: A Life, by Herbert R. Lottman (Little, Brown, 1991), is a painstakingly researched biography of the celebrated French writer and her fascinating life—which included not only writing novels and appearing in cabarets but also dabbling in lesbianism and perhaps even collaborating with the enemy during the Nazi occupation.

THE ARTS   Much of France's beauty can be found in its art. Three books that approach France from this perspective are *The History of Impressionism,* by John Rewald (Museum of Modern Art, 1973), which is a collection of writings about and quotations from the artists, illuminating this period in art; *The French Through Their Films,* by Robin Buss (Ungar, 1988), an exploration of more than 100 widely circulated films; and *The Studios of Paris: The Capital of Art in the Late Nineteenth Century,* by John Milner (Yale University Press, 1988). In the last, Milner presents the dynamic forces that made Paris one of the most complex centers of the art world in the early modern era.

Olympia: Paris in the Age of Manet, by Otto Friedrich (Harper-Collins, 1992), takes its inspiration from the celebrated artwork in the Musée d'Orsay in Paris. From here the book takes off on an anecdote-rich, gossipy chain of historical associations, tracing the rise of the Impressionist school of modern painting, but incorporating social commentary too, such as the pattern of prostitution and venereal disease in 19th-century France.

FICTION The *Chanson de Roland,* edited by F. Whitehead (2nd ed.; Basil Blackwell, 1942), written between the 11th and 14th centuries, is the earliest and most celebrated of the "songs of heroic exploits." *The Misanthrope* and *Tartuffe* (Harcourt, Brace and World, 1965) are two masterful satires on the frivolity of the 17th century by the great comic dramatist Molière. François-Marie Arouet Voltaire's *Candide* (Bantam Classics, 1981) is a classic satire attacking the philosophy of optimism and the abuses of the ancient regime.

A few of the masterpieces of the 19th century are *Madame Bovary,* by Gustave Flaubert (Random House, 1982), in which the carefully wrought characters, setting, and plot attest to Flaubert's genius in presenting the tragedy of Emma Bovary; Victor Hugo's *Les Misérables* (Modern Library, 1983), a classic tale of social oppression and human courage set in the era of Napoleon I; and *Selected Stories* by the master of short stories, Guy de Maupassant (New American Library, 1984).

Honoré de Balzac's *La comédie humaine* (Centre d'Exportation du Livre, Francais, 1999/Original 1831) depicts life in France from the fall of Napoleon to 1848. Henry James's *The Ambassadors* (Penguin USA, 1987/Original 1903) and *The American* (Oxford University Press, 1999/Original 1877) both take place in Paris. *The Vagabond* (Farrar Straus & Giroux, 2001/Original 1978), by Colette, evokes the life of a French music-hall performer.

Tropic of Cancer (Grove Press, 1989/Original 1934) is the semiautobiographical story of Henry Miller's years in Paris. One of France's leading thinkers, Jean-Paul Sartre, shows individuals struggling against their freedom in *No Exit and Three Other Plays* (Vintage Books 1989/Original 1956).

Index

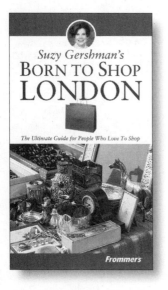
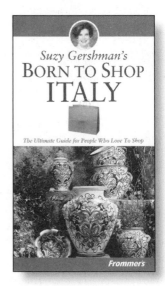

Frommer's® Complete Guides

The only guide independent travelers need to make smart choices, avoid rip-offs, get the most for their money, and travel like a pro.

Frommer's®

®WILEY

Available at bookstores everywhere.

Frommer's® Portable Guides

Destinations in a Nutshell

- Frommer's Portable Acapulco, Ixtapa & Zihuatanejo
- Frommer's Portable Amsterdam
- Frommer's Portable Aruba
- Frommer's Portable Australia's Great Barrier Reef
- Frommer's Portable Bahamas
- Frommer's Portable Berlin
- Frommer's Portable Big Island of Hawaii
- Frommer's Portable Boston
- Frommer's Portable California Wine Country
- Frommer's Portable Cancun
- Frommer's Portable Cayman Islands
- Frommer's Portable Charleston
- Frommer's Portable Chicago
- Frommer's Portable Disneyland®
- Frommer's Portable Dominican Republic
- Frommer's Portable Dublin
- Frommer's Portable Florence
- Frommer's Portable Frankfurt
- Frommer's Portable Hong Kong
- Frommer's Portable Houston
- Frommer's Portable Las Vegas
- Frommer's Portable Las Vegas for Non-Gamblers
- Frommer's Portable London
- Frommer's Portable London from $90 a Day
- Frommer's Portable Los Angeles
- Frommer's Portable Los Cabos & Baja
- Frommer's Portable Maine Coast
- Frommer's Portable Maui
- Frommer's Portable Miami
- Frommer's Portable Nantucket & Martha's Vineyard
- Frommer's Portable New Orleans
- Frommer's Portable New York City
- Frommer's Portable New York City from $90 a Day
- Frommer's Portable Paris
- Frommer's Portable Paris from $90 a Day
- Frommer's Portable Phoenix & Scottsdale
- Frommer's Portable Portland
- Frommer's Portable Puerto Rico
- Frommer's Portable Puerto Vallarta, Manzanillo & Guadalajara
- Frommer's Portable Rio de Janeiro
- Frommer's Portable San Diego
- Frommer's Portable San Francisco
- Frommer's Portable Savannah
- Frommer's Portable Seattle
- Frommer's Portable Sydney
- Frommer's Portable Tampa & St. Petersburg
- Frommer's Portable Vancouver
- Frommer's Portable Vancouver Island
- Frommer's Portable Venice
- Frommer's Portable Virgin Islands
- Frommer's Portable Washington, D.C.